How to Get Lucky

How to Get Lucky

Stacking the Odds in Your Favor
in Life, Love, and Work

by
Sidney Lecker, M.D.
and
Janet Lane Walters

THE BOBBS-MERRILL COMPANY, INC.
Indianapolis/New York

Published by The Bobbs-Merrill Company, Inc.
Indianapolis   New York

Library of Congress Cataloging in Publication Data

Lecker, Sidney.
  How to get lucky.

  1. Success.   I. Title.
BJ1611.2.L43   158'.1   80-681
ISBN 0-672-52660-3

Designed by: Jacques Chazaud
Manufactured in the United States of America
First printing

To My Patients

—S. L.

Contents

How to Get Lucky

1

What Is Luck?

Luck and Laziness

Think about the most treasured things in your life. How did they come about? Did hard work and planning produce your fortunes, or was it blind luck? I'll bet you'll answer, "hard work." But others, viewing your life from the outside, will conclude far more frequently than you would, that luck played a large role in your successes. Don't attribute their conclusions solely to jealousy of your achievements. They just aren't in a position to know how much thought and effort went into your "lucky breaks." If you turn things around and think about how you view the good fortunes of others, you'll find you, too, are susceptible to drawing conclusions with the same bias. You'll admire the great attainments of another person, and, not having been privy to all their advance planning and effort, will conclude that luck played a large, if not a central, role in that person's achievements. The nature of the way we are built psychologically—our inability to understand unless we are told by another what really went into each life event—causes us to draw inaccurate conclusions about cause and effect.

Luck has taken a bad rap for years. It's been equated with passivity, such as in my earlier question, "Did hard work and planning produce your good fortunes, or was it blind luck?" Luck, I have discovered, is anything other than blind. And it's certainly not something that attaches itself to passive people. Let me share with you an experience I had while on a brief vacation in Puerto Rico some years ago.

Up until that vacation, I had always been a person who shunned the gambling tables. I felt I wasn't lucky enough to indulge. Ample prior experience had confirmed this view. Only when I have worked hard at something have I ever succeeded. In the past, when I tried to be lucky, such as in buying a raffle ticket, I was always a loser. I have never won a door prize in my life. Once, at the racetrack during my late teens, I bet on a horse that had been guaranteed by a friend to be a sure winner. As soon as the track announcer shouted excitedly, "They're off!" my horse decided to assert his individuality and he ran right back into the paddock area, taking himself out of the race and making me a sure loser. "If this has been my kind of luck until now, why should I waste my time in a Puerto Rican gambling casino?" I asked myself.

However, my wife of several months was in a mood for excitement, and she refused to let my pessimism spoil her mood. Her what-do-we-have-to-lose-but-money? attitude challenged me to try my luck again. I entered the casino with few hopes, but with a determination not to be a spoilsport.

As I circulated among the gaming tables, which were surrounded by hordes of seemingly obsessed people pushing their money into little slots from which those precious coins rarely reappeared, I once again had a heavy feeling in my chest and the thought that I didn't belong here. This pastime was for compulsive gamblers and losers whom the casino owners were delighted to fleece. Just when I had finished concluding that the house had an insurmountable advantage over the players, I rounded a bend in an aisle between blackjack tables and saw an unusual sight. Sitting there, opposite the dealer, the pit boss, and several off-duty dealers, was one solitary man. His eyes were a combination of squint and smile as he peered over the mountain of multicolored chips piled before him on the table. I later learned that these were one-hundred-dollar tokens. The sight of so much money being bet on every hand was vicariously frightening. By contrast to my timidity, the white-haired man appeared eminently confident. Even more curious was his method of gambling. It was the man against the dealer. No other players shared the table. On some deals, the man asked to play two hands simultaneously. At other times, he asked to be dealt three, four, or five hands, which he played all at once against the lone dealer. The results were as startling as they were consistent. He won the majority of the time. The pit boss changed dealers, but to no avail. The white-haired mystery man with the intense, laughing eyes kept winning . . . and winning . . . and winning.

After a fascinated hour with me as an observer, the game ended. The diminutive man stood up from his victory stool, turned to the pit boss, and made a subtle hand gesture that sent one of the house's assistants scurrying to the cashier's window to convert the mound of tokens into recognizable money. I turned to the white-haired man as he finished counting his stack of one-hundred-dollar bills and asked, "Do you own this hotel?" certain that he had some privileged position at the casino that made everyone cater to his whims, including Lady Luck.

"No, I don't own the hotel . . . but I will, bit by bit," he replied.

On the night following this incident, I watched him gamble once again and he was blessed with the same results. He won big again. I couldn't contain myself. "How did you get so lucky?" I asked boldly.

He took me aside. "Luck has nothing to do with this," he said in a whisper. "I play a system of card counting, and I know when the odds are in my favor. It's at those times that I bet high and play three or four hands. When the cards are against me, I cool it on the bets." He referred me to a book on gambling at blackjack, which I hurried to buy. After I read the book, I knew he was right. Luck played no role whatsoever in his success. Learning how to turn the odds to his advantage was how he had continued to win. And it worked for me in the same way it worked for him as soon as I learned the system. Believe me, it was hard work.

Luck, I learned, is generated in the same way one avoids accidents while driving or flying. Knowing the equipment, keeping it in good order; knowing the Rules of the Road or the Rules of the Sky; and watching out for the other guy are the things you need to know to maintain your lucky streak while driving or flying. The same type of principles apply to gambling at a casino or trying to get a promotion at work. Generating good luck takes work. Hard work. Consistent and persistent effort. That's not for lazy people! Luck doesn't search out the passive or the timid among us. It is chased down by those of us aggressive enough to believe that even luck can be under our control.

Luck and Worthiness

One futile hope of the unlucky is that luck seeks out those who are worthy.

- I'm going to bet the whole bundle. It's about time I won. I deserve it.

- I've had such a bad time in business, it's about time for my ship to come in. I think I'll invest now.

- My last marriage was a washout after so many years. Don't you think it's about time I had a little *mazel?* (Yiddish for "good luck")

Every species of human shares the same myth: "If I'm good, good things will happen to me." This view is heavily sold by all elements of our culture, from religion to school to industry. Yet the truth is otherwise.

- If you're good and perform many good deeds for others, you'll receive your reward in heaven.

- If you work hard, you'll get those grades you need to win acceptance in an Ivy League school. Hard work may not give you the grades which make your admission a sure thing.

- In industry, producers are rewarded with promotion. Good-natured people are admired, but unless they produce they are not advanced.

Success in life has nothing to do with being deserving or having unimpeachable morals. Yet many people subscribe to the view that being worthy has a lot to do with good luck. They believe that patience and morality are the prerequisites of good fortune. Luck, they hold, is akin to taking a number like you do in the neighborhood bakery or butcher shop, and then being patient while waiting for your number to be called. If someone pushes in ahead of you, the just and fair proprietor will refuse to serve that person, and will, instead, call out your number. I'm afraid life doesn't work that way.

Making yourself lucky means not accepting the passive position at the end of the line, nor does it mean shoving yourself ahead of others. It means finding some way you can be served earlier. I hate people who push ahead of me in lines. I am willing to fight to defend my position. When it comes to luck, fighting or pushing ahead doesn't work. Increasing your luck is done by finding a way to avoid the line altogether. Adopting an active position of mastery makes good fortune come your way. Let me give you two examples that demonstrate what I mean.

Because I am a doctor who runs a private practice and a consulting firm as well as being a writer, I don't have much time to spare. I was considering hiring an assistant to do research as well as edit my manuscripts. The mother of one of my patients noticed the books I had written, and she asked me if I needed a ghostwriter. The job I had in mind wasn't that exactly, but I told her that I did need an editorial assistant. She promptly made an appointment to see me, and when she came, she brought samples of her writing. By the next week, the job was hers.

The second example is of a woman I know whose marriage ended unhappily in divorce after sixteen years.

Betty was angry and bitter when I first met her. She resented the fact that men have it all their own way in the divorces of the midlife years. "Who wants a woman with two kids?" she asked. "Look at him. He's dating women ten to fifteen years younger than himself. He acts like he found an eternal fountain of youth out there. Me, I've found humiliation and frustration. It's not fair." As she went on, it became apparent to me that her complaint served as an escape from confronting the difficult task that lay ahead of her—that of rebuilding her life. It was more convenient for her to make remarks about the injustice of the situation than to face the real task.

"First, Betty," I began, "you've told me that you haven't

been able to meet another man. As I've talked to you over the past few weeks, it's become apparent why."

"What do you mean?" she asked, visibly disturbed.

"First you told me that the bar scene was a 'meat market' and you wanted no part of it. Am I right?"

"It's a flesh bazaar . . . degrading and humiliating. Reminds me of the old slave markets or worse. I don't want to get involved in it," she confirmed.

"O.K. . . . so you're not the bar-hopping type. But at another time, you told me how you were once fixed up with a blind date by a friend, and the guy turned out to have four pairs of hands all targeted for your breasts and genitals. Then the next blind date turned out to be an accountant who couldn't decide who was more important in his life—his mother or his analyst."

Betty began to laugh. "You sure have a good memory for the disasters. But they did happen. I'm not sure my friends have any idea what kind of man I'd like."

"Tell me what's left. If you've eliminated bars and blind dates, how will you ever meet a man in today's world? Are you going to sit and wait for Prince Charming to come riding up on his horse? Should we revive the institution of matchmaker for you alone? Are you going to make an application to a computer service?"

Tears filled her eyes. "I deserve a little bit of luck," she shouted. "It's about time after so many years with that husband of mine."

"I agree you deserve better treatment than what's open to you. Bars turn me off, too, and blind dates are like Russian roulette. But that's what's available for meeting dates in our society. You have to play by the rules that exist if you want to win. You can't sit around and bitch about the rules being unfair and that you deserve a better break."

"It's not fair . . . it's just not fair," she muttered through her sobs.

I pressed on. "How many guys do you need?"

Puzzled, she asked, "What do you mean?"

"How many really nice men do you need to make you happy? One, three, five?"

She hesitated for a few minutes. "One . . . I guess."

"There must be hundreds of thousands of eligible men out there from which to pick and choose, and all you need for a life of contentment is one—you need to be a winner only once—and yet you feel victimized by the odds. I think the odds are pretty heavy in your favor. Don't you?"

She smiled. "You're right. In fact, what do I have to lose? I don't have much now. You're telling me to stop sitting and get out there and fight."

Betty is now happily married. The last time I saw her, she smiled and reminded me of our conversation. "I'll never forget your simple point: All I needed was one man . . . the odds were on my side. That single fact alone gave me the courage to go back into the wild world of bars and blind dates. I found Jim. Thanks."

Deserving a lucky break will never make you a winner. Knowing the odds and playing them correctly and fearlessly do.

Luck, Prayer, and Magic

There's no question that some people have far more than their share of good luck. "Let me touch him," you think when you meet one of these people. "Maybe some of his luck will rub off on me." We've all known people who have the Midas touch in business and yet who seem no more intelligent than anyone else. How do they do it? Is it being in the right place at the right time? Is it sheer luck? More often than not, these people have something more working in their favor—and it's not prayer or magic.

What about those people whose lives seem to be just exactly what you'd like yours to be—gratifying, stable, and relaxed? Are they the recipients of divine favors obtained through prayers? Do they have some magic or a clairvoyant power that permits them to see through the confusion of the present into the future and plan better than the rest of us?

We have been told that some people are just plain lucky, and then there are the rest of us who aren't. Some people are born under the right star; the rest are born under a cloud, like the little man in the Li'l Abner comic strip. We are offered magic or prayer, sometimes at a price, to show us how to unlock Heaven's cornucopia. Cunning entrepreneurs vie to sell us a get-rich-quick formula, and we buy. Just read any popular magazine and you'll find out that magic is, indeed, for sale.

- Learn how I bought one million dollars of real estate with no money down. Just send ten dollars for a copy of my book *The Magic of Speculating,* and I'll return your money if you are not perfectly satisfied.

- Want to earn an extra ten thousand, twenty thousand, or thirty thousand dollars *in your spare time?* An investment of only five thousand dollars can put you in the hearing-aid-repair business . . . the one overlooked market that can yield millions of dollars (to the right person). You'll earn unheard-of profits in hearing-aid repairs. Send five dollars for a color brochure on this country's newest franchise, Hearing Aids and Things. You'll start earning money as soon as you learn the secrets of franchise ownership.

Lots of people want to sell you their magic formula for success. Their pitch is that they've been blessed with something that has been denied to you. But, being generous souls, they'll pass the secret along to you, at a price. The fact is that everyone has the same inherent chance of being lucky, since the law of averages works the same for all of us. Those of us who learn to understand the most elementary logic about odds and probability have a leading edge on everyone else. You don't need a master's degree in computer science to know how to work the odds in your favor. Simple common sense is enough. Nobody has anything to sell you that is their sole proprietary magic. Your common sense is as good as theirs. They may simply have learned to use it more aggressively. No prayer will help you bend the odds in your favor, because the laws of probability were incorporated into the grand design from the start. Taking your case to Heaven, where the rules were first made, won't work.

The successful businessperson plays with probability every day. Money is leveraged in order to increase the financial impact of a successful investment. Hedges are put on every bet to insure against disastrous losses by separately incorporating different business projects so that failure of one won't automatically cause the entire financial empire to collapse. A company that is dependent on a seasonal business tries to diversify so it can earn money in the off-season with the same staff and equipment. Winter ski resorts become summer spas when the season changes. Good businesspeople play the odds all the time and win, not because they add prayer to every move or possess magic powers others do not, but because they know good luck is made, not bestowed on us.

Luck in love or in family life is similarly not for sale; it doesn't come through prayer; and it most certainly doesn't rely on a special and rationed magic available only to believers. Every human being is capable of having satisfactory relationships with loved ones and friends. Within every person is the same set of emotional reactions that every other member of the human race possesses. Yet many of us feel that we "just can't communicate with people." We look at our more fortunate counterparts whose social and family lives are more successful and satisfying and believe that they've got a certain something that we are missing. Mother Nature would disagree. She provided each one of us with an adequate complement of emotions and communicative abilities to insure success in interpersonal relationships. However, some of us believe ourselves to be deprived or deficient in these things. So we act like less-fortunate people, and then we get trapped in our own self-fulfilling prophecy. In fifteen years of psychiatric work, I've never met one person whom I could not help to find ways to achieve satisfying emotional relationships if he or she was willing to work at it.

In order to maximize your luck, you must see it as a developed skill, not something that comes from magic or from prayer. You need to think of luck as you think of time: Luck can be used, or it can just be allowed to slip between your fingers. Luck is the currency we all have an equal share of—the Laws of Probability saw to that. But some of us waste our chances; others squeeze every benefit out of every opportunity.

Luck and Probability

- I'm in a batting slump.

- Every investment I've made has gone sour; why should this one be any different?

- I have three bratty kids. I don't want a fourth.

Every one of us has made statements like the ones above at some time or other. We inherently assume that luck runs in strings. "Bad luck comes in threes," we say. "I'm having a run of good luck; that's why I'm going to bet heavily on the next deal that comes along," we reason. The human mind has a big romantic streak when it comes to understanding probability. We believe in invisible cosmic forces that set odds for us, thus giving us runs of good luck and runs of bad luck. In fact, the laws of Nature include the Laws of Probability. And these laws say that each toss of the coin has the same odds as any previous or subsequent one—precisely a 50–50 chance of coming up heads or tails, *no matter how long a string of heads or tails you've been running*. Isn't Mother Nature wonderful? She gives us a chance to renew our lives with every roll of the dice. And we, narrow-minded mortals that we are, look the gift horse in the mouth and assume Nature is pulling our leg. We operate on the assumption that if our luck is bad, we are being punished, and the outcome will continue to be negative until we have appeased the heavens.

Every time a baseball player goes to bat, he is his own worst enemy if he believes that his luck has been preordained. If he is in the throes of a batting slump, the best attitude for him to have is the one based on the statistics: "I can hit a home run any time at bat. Previous strikeouts have nothing to do with my chances right now."

The woman whose love life has been disappointing for years is provided by Mother Nature with new odds every time the woman goes out on a date. "This may be the day Prince Charming will arrive, despite all the previous disappointments I have suffered." Yet we choose to believe our pessimism more than the laws of probability. Hence we assume the worst, and the tension generated by the fear of failure creates the dreaded result.

In this book, we're not going to become engaged in a heavy discussion of mathematics and statistics. Rely on me to play the odds in my favor. I know very little about the science of statistics. But I do know a lot about common-sense tactics that can help maximize the odds in your favor and allow you to acquire, through your own efforts, the good luck you so much desire. I'm not a statistics professor. I am a psychiatrist with a broad background in helping people cope with self-inflicted failures in their lives. I know how to help you clear away the psychological debris of your past failures so that you can play the odds in your favor and get lucky. In this book we'll range from business, to family life, to affairs of the heart, to gambling, to raising children, to retirement, and you'll learn how to strip away pessimism and respond only to the laws of probability. You'll learn strategies that you can apply to every facet of your life that will make you appear lucky to others. The most difficult mathematical concept you'll need to know is: "What are the odds in every flip of a coin?" The answer, of course, is 50–50. If you can add and subtract, you'll have enough mathematical wizardry to understand how to get lucky in all aspects of your life.

2

Stacking the Odds in Your Favor

What Are the Odds?

If you've ever spent time in places where gambling occurs, you will have heard the question, "What are the odds?" asked many times. You may have asked this question yourself without understanding what the answer "20–1"; "3–1"; or "odds even" meant. "I'll spot you 10 points on Team X" is another way of quoting the odds. What do these things mean?

A patient of mine who grew up in a poker-playing family told me that one of her earliest memories involved being told never to draw to an inside straight. Needless to say, because these words were so commonly used, she never thought about

15

what they meant and how they could be applied to anything other than poker. When things went sour in her life, this saying popped into her thoughts and she couldn't shake it. She decided to find out why it was bothering her. A straight in poker is five sequential cards that may or may not be of the same suit—9, 8, 7, 6, 5. An inside straight lacks the middle card—9, 8, 6, 5. The odds are about 43–4 or 11–1 against filling this hand. "That's what I was doing with my life," she said. "Trying to achieve the impossible without ever looking at the odds."

Odds are based on mathematical probabilities. In the above example, to figure the odds, you have to know what kind of numbers you're dealing with. In this case, there are 52 cards in a deck. A poker hand consists of 5 cards, so there are 47 cards you haven't seen. Four of these cards are the needed 7, leaving 43 that aren't. Figuring the odds in this case is relatively simple, but with the odds in other areas, many factors must be considered before these odds can be calculated. Let's look at two women who started businesses. One succeeded because she calculated the odds, while the other failed even to see that there were any odds. The success story first, so you can practice seeing where the second woman failed to realize the odds.

For six years, Margery had taught nursing on the college level, and each year she was excessed in May, only to be rehired in September. "The last time it happened, I decided I'd had enough of this planned uncertainty. I had my master's degree, and I didn't want to return to hospital nursing, so I began to evaluate possible futures in my chosen career. I wanted to find something where I could have some control over what was happening to me. These are few and far between."

Margery decided to open a nurse's registry that would supply private-duty nurses to individuals, and also would supply fill-in nurses for hospitals and doctor's offices when they were short-staffed or during vacations. After deciding on what she would do, she began to plan how she would go about achieving success. She investigated regulations for licensing this type of agency before she committed herself to this course of action. Then she talked to a friend who had a great deal of business experience and who she knew was tired of her job as an office manager, which gave her responsibility without salary or prestige. They decided to set up a partnership, and that's when the real planning began. They found there were quite a few agencies that supplied nurses and other home-care personnel. They also learned that these agencies often had trouble with staffing because of the high commissions they charged their nurses. Margery and her partner decided on a policy of charging their nurses a small fee and collecting the bulk of their service fees from the clients.

First Margery and her friend had to decide on an area in which to locate their new business. They finally decided to settle where there was a high concentration of money, realizing that people who have money are willing and able to hire private-duty nurses when they are sick. Then they chose an office location. For this purpose, they selected a building that catered to doctors, and they rented an office there. After they rented the office, they received their license from the state. They also set aside in a special account enough money to cover their office expenses for a year, and an additional amount to pay the nurses they would hire until insurance and private payments began to arrive.

Margery made a point of introducing herself to the doctors in the building and those in the surrounding area. She left pamphlets explaining the services the agency offered. Her partner called the area hospitals and informed them that they would have nurses available for relief duty. They advertised in the local newspapers for nurses, and were careful to hire only those with recent experience so they could assure quality care to their clients. They arranged an orientation day with the local hospitals so their nurses would be aware of the differences in policy, and they taught their nurses how to fill out insurance forms. During the first year, Margery often filled in as the need for nurses arose and she was unable to supply one. She and her partner were careful not to accept clients if they knew they couldn't supply a nurse.

The first year saw Margery sometimes working seven days a week, and occasionally her days were sixteen hours long. All this for less than she had been earning as a nursing instructor. A lot of people shook their heads and told her she was crazy. But she was willing to do this because she knew it increased her odds for success. Her partner also worked long hours and had a phone installed in her home so she could take calls for nurses at times when she wasn't at the office. Their reputation for quality care and excellent nurses began to spread. Last year was the second full year of business, and Margery and her partner earned salaries of thirty thousand dollars each. They are now opening a second office in another high-money-concentration area.

Margery used a number of winning strategies as she assessed the odds and used them for success. Let's see what they were:

- When she decided to take a partner, Margery was using the Principle of Minimax.

- When she selected her partner, she was using the Compatibility Quotient.

- When she chose her location and set aside money in a special account, Margery was exercising the Law of Supply and Demand.

- When she explained the service to the local doctors and when her partner called the area hospitals, they were using the Rule of Need.

- When they investigated the regulations for receiving a license, they were learning the Rules of the Game.

- When the decision was made to charge small fees to the nurses they hired, Margery and her partner were employing the Human Factor.

The second woman, Rita, was a friend of one of my employees. She lives in a town of about forty thousand people that is near a large city in another state. Rita is a talented writer and a germinator of ideas. Many of the local service organizations like the "Y" and the United Fund used her talents to develop publicity campaigns for them while she was an amateur. She became a success, but she was never paid for her work. The owner of the local advertising agency offered her a partnership in his small, solid advertising agency, but encouraged by the praise she received from her nonpaying customers, she turned the offer down. "I want to be my own boss," she said. So she set up her own public-relations business.

Another friend who also had some experience in the field wanted to join Rita, but the friend had no money to invest. Rita hired her for a small salary, plus a commission for each of the campaigns she worked on and for each of the new clients she brought into the firm. With just a few months' expense money in the bank, Rita opened an office and hired a secretary to handle the phone calls and typing.

Rita expected the organizations for which she had donated her services to keep her on and pay her. These people had praised her skills and talents, but they found less talented amateurs to continue Rita's outlined campaigns. A few small businesses purchased her services, and through hard work she gained some medium-sized businesses as clients. At the end of three months, she was forced to take a bank loan to cover her operating expenses when her savings ran out.

About six months after she started her business, Rita obtained a customer who would bring in nearly a million dollars' worth of business in the next five years. Rita wanted to devote her time to this client, so she let her friend, Connie, handle all the smaller accounts. Three months later, a strike took place in her big customer's business, causing him to cancel the rest of the five-year plan she had set up. Connie left her and set up a rival public-relations firm. Connie took with her most of the small clients, as well as the plans for a number of other campaigns she and Rita had worked out.

Rita's strategies for winning turned out to be not very successful. She ignored most of the winning strategies that Margery had used. Let's see what Rita ignored.

- When Rita turned down the partnership offer and began her own business, she ignored the Principle of Minimax.

- By not being sure she would obtain business from the service organizations, and by not setting aside sufficient running capital, she failed to see the Law of Supply and Demand.

- In her choice of Connie as an employee and in her failure to keep tabs on Connie, she forgot about the Human Factor and the Compatibility Quotient.

- By not assessing possible clients and laying ground work before she plunged into business, Rita ignored the Rule of Need.

- By not covering herself against the loss of clients to Connie, and by not seeing ways to protect herself against the loss of revenue because of the strike, Rita showed that she hadn't learned the Rules of the Game.

Margery's and Rita's strategies for winning were nearly opposite. One succeeded and the other failed. Margery looked at the odds and decided to stack them in her favor. Rita trusted to luck. Margery learned the Rules of the Game before she began, while Rita tried to learn them as she went along. In setting up her services, Margery used the Rule of Need. She worked diligently, while Rita used this rule on a part-time basis. By effectively calculating the Law of Supply and Demand, Margery was in the right place at the right time. Rita wasn't. Rita ignored the Human Factor in her dealings with her employee, Connie, while Margery used this, as well as the Compatibility Quotient, further to stack the odds in her favor. Finally, Margery saw how the odds could be changed by using the Principle of Minimax. Rita ignored this and assumed all the risks.

Margery stacked the odds in her favor by using the six winning strategies. You too can learn to do the same and succeed in your business or marriage or in any other area of life by using the same six winning strategies.

Stacking the Odds

One assumption many people make is that the odds are always against them. This is true with many forms of gambling, and yet people continue to invest heavily in those games that are the most strongly stacked against them. They talk about "The day my ship comes in," or that "Someday, Lady Luck will shine on me." The person who appears lucky is often the person who understands the odds.

Many people play the numbers, and they very seldom win. The real winners in the numbers game are the people who take the bets. That's because they control the odds. To win on the numbers, you must select a combination of digits—perhaps 3.

In this case, there are 10 digits used (0, 1, 2, 3, 4, 5, 6, 7, 8, 9). A combination would be 000, 001, 011, 010, and so forth. When the possible combinations are computed, your chances of picking the winning combination are about 1,000 to 1. Not good odds at all. You stand a better chance of winning at poker or blackjack because you can learn to compute the odds and therefore control your betting in relation to these odds. A good player knows his odds and he drops out when he realizes these odds are stacked against him.

- How can anyone figure the odds? They're always changing.

- If I had a computer, I'd be able to figure the odds. That's what it takes these days.

These two sentiments are often used by people when speaking about the odds. People who appear to be lucky are the ones who have learned to calculate the odds. Most of these people don't have access to computers. Some of them appear to operate on instincts, but what they've done is train themselves to see all the possible factors that can influence success or failure. This has become, for them, an automatic process. After they discover these factors, they assess the effects and calculate the odds.

One of the techniques successful people use is the Principle of Minimax. This can be stated as: "Assume the minimum risks with the maximum results." Taking a partner would be one way to use this technique. If this is done, the risk of loss would be reduced by 50 percent. Then it would be logical to assume that each partner would produce equally, thus increasing the possible productivity. This can as much as double the chances of success than if you would continue to operate alone.

Before you dash out and grab the first person you see to be your partner, there's another assessment that has to be made.

That's called the Compatibility Quotient. Nothing can destroy a new business quicker than two people going in opposite directions. The same goes for any relationship, such as marriage. The elastic cord of partnership will snap with abruptness when partners are incompatible. To assess this factor, you need to look at your own and the other person's goals, values, and methods of action. When you're taking on a partner, ask yourself the following questions:

- Do we work well together?

- Are our goals mutual?

- Do we have similar values?

- Do our methods of acting and taking action complement each other, or are they too much alike?

Partnerships work only when two people are able to work together on a daily or at least a regular basis. If someone you think might be a good partner has little habits that drive you up the wall, find someone else. In a matter of weeks or months, you'll be at each other's throats. If you take on a partner who has a totally different goal for your business or relationship than you do, it's not going to work. Once again, a fight will soon break the partnership in two. Values are your particular moral structures. Becoming a partner to someone who is materialistic while you are altruistic could result in an explosion. If you and your partner are too much alike, you can also lose out because you both are thinking and wanting to do the same things while other areas of the business or partnership are neglected. Choose someone for a partner who is sure to see the things you might forget.

Next comes the Law of Supply and Demand. Obviously, you wouldn't successfully market a diaper service in a community dominated by senior citizens. There's no demand there. You'd be amazed at how many skilled businesspeople ignore this law with catastrophic results. Anyone want to buy my 450-horsepower Buick that gets 6 miles to the gallon? Simply stated, the Law of Supply and Demand says that when there is a need, someone will step in to fill it. This person could be you, or you can learn to create new needs to alter the odds in your favor.

The odds of winning in business and in life in general are influenced by the Rule of Need. Needs may be inherent or they may be created. Food, clothing, and shelter are inherent needs, while watching television and buying designer clothes are created needs. In business, you can stack the odds in your favor by finding a way to create a need for your product or supply.

When you are trying to stack the odds in your own favor, the Human Factor must always be considered. How do people react? How can their interest be captured? What are their patterns of interaction, and how can you capitalize on these things? How many times have your plans been dynamited by the actions or reactions of others?

The final way of assessing and stacking the odds is by learning the Rules of the Game you're playing. No matter what your situation in life is, certain rules exist for success. In everything you do, having the rules down pat and working them to your advantage put you ahead.

An acquaintance of mine has a seventeen-year-old son who has earned a tidy sum of money in the past year by betting on the World Series and the Super Bowl. What was amazing was that he won it all by bets of one dollar and two dollars. He won forty-five dollars on the World Series and sixty-five dollars on the Super Bowl by betting with his classmates. Although I don't condone gambling by teen-agers, this young man's strategies showed he knew how to stack the odds in his favor. Here's how he did it.

This young man has a good understanding of both baseball and football, especially the statistical end of the game. For a term paper, he did a study of artificial turf as opposed to natural turf, and the effects of artificial turf on hitting and fielding.

When asked why he chose small bets, he replied, "That's what my friends can afford. Sure, I'd like to bet big, but then I'd have no one to bet with." (That's employing the Rule of Need.) He also created an image of himself as someone who pays off a losing bet immediately. He expects the same from those who bet with him. And if someone doesn't pay up, he won't bet with him again, no matter what odds they want to give him. A lot of his peers think he's lucky, and they bet with him thinking they'll be the one to break his lucky streak. Everyone wants to be the one to beat the top gun to the draw.

When I asked this boy why he picked the Pirates in the World Series when most of the experts were going with Baltimore, he admitted it was partly out of sentiment. "I really wouldn't let that get in the way, though, if I hadn't thought the Pirates had a better team. They had this family thing, which a lot of people laughed at, but it gave them an edge when they were down. They had a better offensive team than Baltimore, and in a short series of games, hitting usually tells. The Pirates weren't a bad team defensively either."

"What about the Super Bowl? I understand you gave those betting against the Steelers 11 points. The final score showed the Steelers 12 points ahead. Many of the experts were going with 12.5 or 13 points."

He laughed. "I looked at the offensive and defensive records of both teams. I took the points the Steelers had scored and compared them with the points the Rams had scored against the other teams. I did the same with the points scored against the two teams. I subtracted the results and came up with a 13-point differential that the Steelers would win by. *Then I knocked off 2 points for assurance so the odds were on my side.* I turned down bets where the bettor wanted a bigger spread."

Then he added, "I'd never go to Las Vegas like my parents do. I'd be on the wrong side of the odds. I don't know enough about that kind of gambling. I'd have to do a lot of studying before I went."

In making the odds work for him, this enterprising young man used many of the winning strategies. Let's look at the ones he used.

- He learned the Rules of the Games he was betting on and was able to use this knowledge to calculate the odds.

- When choosing the Steelers and deciding on the limits of money he would bet, he looked at the Human Factor.

- He employed the Rule of Need when he decided to limit his bets to what his classmates could afford.

- He discovered a use for the Principle of Minimax when he knocked off two points after he calculated the odds.

- He followed the Law of Supply and Demand when he chose to bet with his classmates.

By applying these effective strategies, this young man did something few other people did.

The Odds and Hunches

Some people seem to control the odds in a magical way. They are always talking about playing their hunches. Just what are they talking about, and are hunches magic, or are they another way of using the odds?

- "It was just a hunch," said the man who bought the land that he later sold to the airport for expansion.

- Four years ago, something told me to buy gold. I guess you might say I had a hunch. I really can't remember why I bought it.

Many people have hunches, but few people take risks based on these hunches. What really is a hunch? And what should you do when you have one: ignore it? investigate it? or take a flier?

The man who bought the land near the airport may have observed that air traffic was increasing. This observation probably didn't register consciously. The mind is a fabulous computer that silently registers fantastic quantities of information. When the land went up for sale, this man, ordinarily not a land speculator, had a hunch. He took a flier on the land, not realizing that six million brain cells he possessed had unconsciously computed the odds and sent a message to his conscious mind. "Buy that land" was the message that registered in his mind. It felt like a hunch, but in reality, it was the product of deep, unconscious calculations.

What about the man who bought the gold on a hunch? He may have realized that gold is a good long-term investment, or perhaps something he read about the instability of the world monetary system began to nag at him. He may have had a good reason for buying gold without looking into the why. Of course, when the gold market skyrocketed, he had already bought gold and he made a fortune. His hunch was really a series of unconscious conclusions. Learning to capitalize on these unconscious conclusions made by your mind can substantially improve your luck.

How do you know which of your hunches are based on vital unconscious knowledge? How do these hunches affect the odds? If you can bring this hidden knowledge to the surface, you can add it to your reasons for choosing a particular course of action.

You may also find that when you stop to analyze a hunch and look for further data, your memory has played you false. You may have misheard or misseen, partially heard or partially seen, or misinterpreted what you heard or saw. A good example of this can be noted when a number of witnesses describe an accident. There may be as many different reports of an accident as there are witnesses. If this is the case, how can you trust your hunches?

A friend of mine has a close friend, Tom, who has a small jewelry manufacturing company. He just opened his shop in a new location, and he invited my friend to see it. While she was there, she noticed the earrings his wife was wearing. The gold earrings were unusual, plain, and sophisticated. Rather than being flat, they gave the impression of being three-dimensional. "You should design a line of earrings like that and engrave them," she said.

Tom laughed. "They're just earrings."

When my friend went home, the thought of those earrings continued to nag her. Why do I feel this way about them? she wondered. They're gold, and I remember how impressed I was by the King Tut exhibition. I did a lot of reading about gold jewelry then. She smiled. What's wrong with engraving them? Monograms are a snob thing, and so is gold jewelry. Look at the people who wear designer's monogrammed items. Just think what an impact it would be if you could have your own monogrammed jewelry.

With great determination, she worked out a program which included samples of advertisements which could be used to sell these earrings. Why stop with earrings? she thought. Bracelets and necklaces with that design would be nice. When she finished the program, she called Tom and went to see him. They spent three hours going over the plans, and Tom began to react with enthusiasm. He's going to put that design and four others they worked out that Sunday afternoon in his line for next Christmas. Best of all, he's given my friend a 10 percent interest in the line for the use of her ideas in selling this jewelry.

My friend had a hunch, but she didn't stop there. The first thing she did was mention this to someone who laughed at it. Instead of being daunted by the negative response, she went home and worked on her hunch. She discovered where her idea had come from. She thought about women's responses to jewelry and the snob appeal of monograms. Then she did some further reading about gold jewelry and discovered there never was a time when it wasn't in fashion. Next she took her hunch and used the material she had gained from research to work out a systematic program that would use the idea and the information. She presented Tom with her carefully worked-out package, and this time he listened, because her idea now was based on more than a hunch.

Immediately after the Second World War, a small building contractor who lived near Pittsburgh bought land that had been part of a strip mine. Many people laughed and wondered why anyone would want this barren land. His response was that he had a hunch. There was more to what he did than a hunch. He had seen how this land could be used to bring himself a profit. He saw that when the war was over, many veterans would be returning home and there would be an upswing in marriage. New families need homes, so he began building small houses that could be purchased at reasonable prices. This man had an idea and he put it to work. Because he listened to his original hunch and made plans, he became a millionaire.

A good rule to remember is: "Hunches aren't magic bolts out of the blue. They are ideas that should be explored and tested against your knowledge of the odds." When you have a hunch, ask yourself the following questions:

- What data in my unconscious is this idea based on?

- Is it based on information I have heard, read, or seen?

- Is this information true or false? Could I have misunderstood or misinterpreted what I read, heard, or saw?

- How can I prove my hunch has a solid base?

- Can I work out a usable plan based on my hunch and my research?

- How can I change the odds involved in my idea by applying the six winning strategies?

After you have answered these questions, you are ready to put your plan into action.

Changing and Using the Odds

Suppose you have met the most wonderful man or woman in the world and your hunch tells you to marry him or her. After reading about the marriage and divorce statistics, you aren't sure you want to take the plunge. You've read that nearly one out of two marriages ends in divorce. Instead of shrugging your shoulders and deciding to stay single for the rest of your life, you could look instead into the idea of marriage and its potential stability from a personal angle.

The statement about the divorce rate is true, as far as it goes. But it ignores the fact that the odds are more in favor of a marriage surviving if it's a first marriage. These odds are for one in four of these marriages ending in divorce. Already your chances have improved. Then you read that if you live in

California, the odds for a marriage ending in divorce are greater than those in your home state of Iowa. Once again, your chances have improved. Next check the divorce statistics for people who have chosen the same career as you and your potential mate. What about religious preference and divorce? By checking the statistics you may discover that the chances of your contemplated marriage succeeding are excellent.

What you can learn from not giving up is that there is more than one way of looking at the odds when you're applying them to your specific problem. Make sure you know all the facts behind the odds before you use them to make a decision.

To change the odds, you have to test their validity. You need to look at your hunches and apply the winning strategies. The odds may be in your favor; they may be even; or you could even be playing a long shot. Even when the odds seem to be against you, they may be better than you think. Let's look at how you could apply these things in your own life.

While talking to a friend, you hear how he or she went to Las Vegas and won. This fascinates you because you know this friend is about as lucky as you are, which isn't saying much. "How did you do it?" you ask, and you think, "If he can do it, so can I." You've just had a hunch.

"I was doing badly," said your friend. "Then I heard about this book. I ran to the bookstore and bought it. That whole day, I spent studying the basic strategy in that book, and in the evening, I returned to the casino. I followed the strategy, and to my surprise, it worked. I didn't win big sums of money, but I snapped my losing streak and won back most of the four hundred dollars I had lost."

"I wonder if I could do the same thing?" you think. "I have money in the bank for a vacation, and just maybe . . ." You ask, "What's the name of the book? Could I borrow it?"

Two days later, your friend brings you the book. You go home and begin studying. You would like to go to Las Vegas; it's been a dream of yours to win at gambling, but you know how your luck has been when you've played cards at home with friends. You've also heard that the odds are with the house in Las Vegas. This means they're against you, and this idea turns you off. If there is a way you can turn those odds around, you know you could have a good time.

Before you can use the odds, you have to know how to judge what the odds are in any given case. To do this, you must gather your data from as many sources as possible. You must look at your hunch or dream to see what it really involves. Then you must find ways to employ the six winning strategies. Finally you will again look at the odds and flow with them.

After you read the book on gambling, you are ready to see if your hunch about going to Las Vegas is valid or not. When you read the book, you discovered that blackjack gives you the best chance of winning in a casino. You're not going to trust to luck, because that's what the casinos expect you to do.

What you have done so far is to have a dream or a hunch and to look at the odds. Now you are ready to see if you can change those odds to favor yourself. To do this, you'll have to employ the six winning strategies.

The Compatibility Quotient is the first technique to employ in this case. If you don't like playing cards, or if you think negatively about gambling, you won't be very compatible with blackjack or any other casino game. If this is the case, you should think of another place to spend your vacation. But you decide that you are compatible with the idea of playing blackjack.

The next step when playing blackjack or any other gambling game is to learn the Rules of the Game. In blackjack, you're trying to beat the dealer by getting a better hand than he does without going over 21 points. You'll need to learn the value points of the cards in order to do this. Once you've mastered the Rules of the Game, you'll need to learn the strategies. The object of learning the rules and strategy behind the play of the game is so you can play each hand the right way, oddswise. In this way, you'll have a slight edge rather than having the odds stacked against you. A slight edge is all you'll need to have an enjoyable time and perhaps come home with a little money.

Next, look at the Rule of Need. What are your reasons for wanting to gamble? Perhaps it's to pit your skill against that of another person. Maybe it's for excitement, or for fun, but knowing your reasons will help you when you sit down at the gaming table. As you play, it's important for you to remember why you're playing.

The Law of Supply and Demand comes next. To follow this, you should keep in mind that you should play within the limits of your pocketbook. It's very human to panic if you're afraid you'll lose the money you've already allocated for something else—say, for your meals the next day. It's also human to think, "This can't happen to me." If you don't have the money, don't play. You may be tempted to take unwise risks. You must be able to supply comfortably what someone else will demand— your money, if you lose.

The Human Factor comes into play when you go to a casino. If the presence of noise interferes with your ability to concentrate, you'll have difficulty here. This is one way casinos stack the odds on their side. Practice concentrating in the midst of chaos before you go. When you are at the casino, look for a game where there are two other players. Too many players change the odds. Observe the players and choose the quiet group. There's nothing worse for concentration than the presence of a chatterer, a complainer, or a loud, drunken boor. It's also a good idea not to drink, as this can disturb another Human Factor—you and your ability to concentrate.

The Principle of Minimax will have an important effect on whether you win or lose. Remember, it's minimum risks with maximum success. The best way to insure this is to follow all the steps listed above, and stick to them. Even if you're tempted in the heat of the game to go against the strategies, *don't*. When you do, you'll be changing the odds away from your favor.

As you can see, the odds can be made to work for you rather than for the other person. It will take work on your part instead of depending on luck. As you work and study the odds, you'll begin to appear lucky to others, and they'll think the odds are on your side. They will be because you have employed them that way.

3

The Lucky
Frame of Mind

When Opportunity Knocks

Every day, you are surrounded by a multitude of opportunities. But only when these opportunities are compatible with your mode of expression are you able to take advantage of them. What may be an opportunity to you may not be one for your next-door neighbor, and vice versa. If you're not a writer, you could walk past an almost complete story and not recognize it. On the other hand, a writer could easily miss an opportunity to make a fortune on the stock market. The ways many people miss out on opportunities are often for totally different reasons. How often have you said,

"Why didn't I think of that?" or "I thought about that, but I never dreamed it would get off the ground."

Susan is an art teacher who would like to quit teaching and spend a few years painting and building her reputation as an artist. Unfortunately, she likes to eat and have a roof over her head. She needs to have some money in the bank before she can give up her job. While looking around for a way to make extra money, she investigated a number of possibilities. Then one day, she was in a local needlepoint store, and she overheard a woman say, "None of these canvases are what I really want. I know what pattern I want for my dining-room chairs, but I can't draw and I can't even find anything close." Susan introduced herself to the woman and told her she was an artist. She offered to paint the canvases for the woman. This first commission led to others, and Susan is well on the way to having enough money in the bank so she can follow her dream.

The opportunity you missed doesn't have to concern the invention of something new. It can be an adaptation of an old idea or a way to do something better. While many people give Henry Ford credit for inventing the automobile, that wasn't his function in the industry. He invented the techniques for mass production that gave us all a chance to own a car.

One of the keys to a lucky frame of mind is your ability to see an opportunity. Do you look in another direction if an opportunity approaches? Do you walk around it and view it from all angles? Are you blind to the presence of opportunities? The person who successfully seizes opportunities is a person who has cultivated a diamond cutter's eye. Before a diamond cutter strikes his first blow to free a diamond from its rough enclosure, he studies it from all angles. Only when he is sure he won't destroy the gem does he pick up his hammer and strike. You can't do this with an opportunity unless you know one when you see one.

Joe, a psychiatrist I know, failed to recognize an opportunity to enhance his reputation, not to mention his pocketbook. One of the top psychiatrists in the country offered this man a chance to work part-time in his office. All Joe could see was the extra work this would mean for him, and he turned it down. When he complained to me about how bad his luck was, I shook my head. Luck, good or bad, had nothing to do with his failure to advance in the field. Joe hadn't cultivated the diamond cutter's eye. Opportunity knocked and he looked the other way.

Jody got in on the ground floor of a new drafting firm. She began as a secretary-receptionist, and after ten years, while the firm has grown, Jody still holds the same position. There are now an office manager and eight secretaries, all hired after Jody. When she came to see me, she was depressed. "I just don't get the breaks," she said. "Karen was hired two years after I was and now she's the office manager. When Mr. Slade needed a private secretary, he chose Laura. She's only been there five years. I come to work every day and do my job, but nothing good ever happens to me."

"What have you done to change this?" I asked. "You must have known these changes were going to take place."

"I do my job," she said. "I don't go poking around or getting involved in office gossip. They should have offered me one of those jobs. Karen went in and suggested they needed an office manager. I could have told them the same thing, but no one asked me."

Jody never moved ahead because she held herself aloof from what was happening. She had developed a form of blindness to opportunity. The person who moves ahead is always looking and listening because he or she knows that an opportunity for advancement may occur at any time.

Karen, Jody's fellow worker, was someone who saw an opportunity developing. Instead of waiting for it to come to her, she found an opening and went after it.

Seeing opportunity has a lot to do with your mental attitudes. If you haven't cultivated a diamond cutter's eye, you may fit the description I once heard a man give to a fellow worker. "He wouldn't know an opportunity if it walked up and hit him over the head. And if it did, he'd stand there and stare, or he'd start taking action, but always in the wrong direction."

Once you have recognized an opportunity, your reaction to it is important. Do you fight, or do you freeze? Both of these reactions are common, and knowing how you react initially can help you plan your strategies for dealing with the opportunities that surround you.

When Jean came into my office, she was in a panic state. "I can't do anything," she said. "It's like I'm afraid to move or to breathe. I almost called to cancel because I didn't want to leave the house."

Jean had just begun a new job as a ghostwriter, and she was faced with what is known as "writer's block." Although she has been writing for years, and has had some small successes, she has just been given a contract to write a book. This contract involves a large sum of money, and it is one that can bring her prestige. This assignment was one of those "opportunities you can't afford to miss." Jean literally couldn't sit at her typewriter without becoming ill. What Jean was doing was responding to her big chance by a pattern of flight. She wanted to succeed, but she was afraid she would fail, so she froze.

"Why can't you write?" I asked. "You're not a novice."

"I know that, but I can't help thinking about everything that could go wrong—and I mean everything. Things like, what happens if the book bombs? What if my typewriter broke? What if I broke my arms?"

"Don't you think it's about time you stopped inventing problems and got to work?" I asked. "You're getting too far ahead of yourself. Already you're worried about the book being a failure and you haven't even started writing it."

Jean looked at me. "You're right." Then she smiled. "I always react this way, but this time, I couldn't stop myself. I'm usually able to put a rein on my imagination and settle down to work. . . . You know, I'm going home and start writing. If I'm really into the book, I'll have to cancel next Tuesday's session with you."

"You're getting ahead of yourself again," I warned. "Wait until Monday morning before you decide to cancel."

Following our session, Jean was ready to stop her flight and start fighting. She had regained her balance.

Peter, on the other hand, reacts by fighting. When he is faced with something new, or a decision, he comes out of his corner with his fists raised. He generally wastes a lot of time trying to mop up the opportunities he's shattered because he's not discriminating about when or what he fights. His attitude is that nothing can go wrong if you're willing to fight. Peter's problem is that he doesn't know when to stop fighting.

In order to cultivate the lucky frame of mind, you need to know:

- How to recognize opportunities.

- How you react to opportunities.

- How to turn an opportunity into a reality.

If any of these mental processes is missing when opportunity knocks, you may open the door to disaster.

Cultivating Opportunity Insight

When a gardener gets ready to plant a garden, he analyzes the soil to see if any minerals that are necessary for the growth of his plants are missing. If there are, he supplies them. In the same way, you have to check your modes of thinking to see if there are any missing. You need to be able to employ broad-scope, fine-detail, vertical, horizontal, left-brain, right-brain, and contrary thinking in order to recognize and capitalize on opportunities. The people who seem lucky are able to use all of these types of thought patterns and to synchronize them. They have developed a diamond cutter's eye. With practice and through the use of a number of techniques, you can also learn to develop and use your mind like a diamond cutter.

Marsha is an interior decorator, but this isn't what she started out to be. She studied art with a major in painting. Over the past twenty years, Marsha has developed an unusual talent. From a myriad of small items, she is able to make a room into something special and unique. She teaches a course in interior decorating, and she often repeats this advice to her students. "First, you have to see all the details, and then, in your mind, you have to put them together to see if they make a whole. You may find that one small item, such as a vase, doesn't fit, but when you remove it, you have a complete picture. At other times, you may visualize something is missing, and your picture of the room isn't complete. It takes a lot of practice before this skill becomes effortless."

Marsha is successful at interior decorating, and she is also successful as an artist. Her skills for interior decorating were discovered by a "fortunate accident." When a friend bought a new house, Marsha took one of her paintings to the friend's nearly empty house as a housewarming gift. As she toured the new house, she began to tell her friend how each room should look. Her friend decided to decorate by re-creating what Marsha had told her. When she finished the living room, she invited Marsha over. The room didn't seem quite right to Marsha, so she moved a picture, shifted a chair and two lamps, and the room was right. Her friend told other people about this skill of Marsha's, and soon Marsha was in business. When Marsha works on a room or a house, she uses broad-scope and fine-detail thinking.

Broad-scope thinking deals with a completed picture.

When you become skilled in this type of thinking, you can visualize wholeness or completeness. But if you employ this kind of thinking without employing its opposite—fine-detail thinking—you may create an amorphous mass. You're seeing the forest, but not the trees. Or you could be seeing the trees and not seeing the branches and the leaves. To have your picture mean something, you have to know the details are there. If they aren't, you'll be in the shoes of the man who set out to establish a successful company, but who forgot to think of such details as capital, location, customers, and employees. The following exercises will help you gain this ability for dual thinking.

- Take a small tray and place five round objects on the tray. Use such things as a ball of yarn, a coin, an orange, a plate, and a coaster. After you've studied it, go into another room and draw a picture of the tray and its contents. Your artwork doesn't matter. Now, add five square objects to the tray in random fashion. Go to the other room and again draw the tray and its objects. Finally add five cylindrical items such as a glass, a tube of lipstick, etc. Return to the other room and again make a drawing of the tray and items. When you are making your sketch, try to visualize the whole picture and then add the details.

- Another good exercise is to take a room in your house or apartment (one you can't see from where you are sitting) and make a sketch of that room, trying to put in all the details you can. Then take your sketch and visit that room. How much did you leave out?

- Have someone remove an item from your

living room and see how long it takes you to spot the missing item. A picture that hung in my living room for three years was removed for reframing. While I knew something was missing, it was nearly twenty minutes before my mind told me it was the picture. I was seeing the forest and ignoring the trees.

• An exercise that is often used in creative-writing classes can help you synthesize details into wholeness. It consists of reading a short story up to the last page or two. Then you complete the story in your own way. Compare your ending with the author's. Was your version completely different? Now go back and read the story with the author's ending. Can you see how he completed the picture? Repeat this exercise with different stories.

• The final exercise is to look at the world around you and select an opportunity. Newspapers and magazines abound with opportunities, but I'm not suggesting you go out and invest in one of these. This is a paper investment. After you've selected the opportunity, decide on what this completed business will be like. Plan every detail needed to make this a success.

When you have completed these exercises, you will have access to two ways of thinking that will help you discover and use the opportunities around you. You're now ready to practice two more ways of thinking.

Larry is a church organist. He has just received an offer from a new church. He has held his present position for seven years. As he examines this new opportunity, he first looks at salary, hospitalization, pension benefits, and the organ he will be playing, and contrasts them with those of his present job. If he stops here in his explorations, he will have used just vertical thinking, and he will be seeing only what is in front of him. Before he makes a decision, he should look horizontally. He needs to examine the peripheral benefits. When he does this, he finds that the new church offers him a chance for professional growth. When he began his present job, there was a choir nucleus, but at the new church, there is no choir. While he has built on the existing choir program, he has never planned and designed a choir program from scratch. He also sees that he has taken his present choir about as far as it will go and he's now coasting. In order to make his decision about his career he now can use both vertical and horizontal thinking.

Vertical thinking is seeing what's in front of you. It involves the obvious and is very literal. While vertical thinking can provide you with reams of data, it ignores the periphery. This sideways kind of thinking is horizontal. It's the kind of thinking that can see the side effects and benefits, good as well as bad. The following exercises are designed to help you develop these two kinds of thinking.

- "What if " is a good exercise to practice. Select a subject, such as elephants. Then follow this pattern. "An elephant is gray, but what if an elephant were blue?" Answer your question. "It would be invisible when flying unless it was a cloudy day." And so forth. When you are using this exercise, first state the obvious, and follow this with a question that looks around the corner. Children are great with this type of thinking.

- In this second exercise, take someone or something you know fairly well—say, yourself. First state all the obvious facts. "I am 5 feet, 10 inches tall. My hair is brown and my eyes are hazel. I weigh 175 pounds, but there is too much gathered in my middle." When you have listed all the vertical data, look at the horizontal information. "The reason I have extra weight around my middle is because I don't have time for exercise. I am a serious person who often has trouble telling when people are teasing. I try to hide my emotions from others. I have difficulty delegating authority." After you've explored your subject in both directions, you have a better picture in your mind. You can repeat this exercise with a variety of subjects.

• "Let's pretend" is another good exercise for vertical and horizontal thinking. Let's pretend you are going to open a music store. Make two columns on a piece of paper and employ horizontal and vertical thinking. In one column, labelled "Vertical," list the *obvious* items and/or services your store might provide. In a column labelled "Horizontal," list those that are *not* so obvious. For example:

Vertical	*Horizontal*
sheet music	T-shirts
records	music lessons
tapes	vocal coaching
instruments	music-related
	art items

After your list is complete, visit a music store and see what you missed. You can, of course, choose any type of business for playing this game.

When Marcy was divorced, she came to the realization that she needed a job that would earn her a steady income. She has a degree in English and was a selling writer of fiction, but not for large sums of money. "I want to keep on writing," she said. "But I can't afford to sit around and wait for a best seller. An editor friend just offered me a job in his publishing company. It makes sense to take it, but frankly I'm scared. I know about the creative side of writing, but the practical end of the business is a total mystery. I've never been interested in things like costs (I never paid the bills until after the divorce) or all the details that go into producing a finished book. That's what an editor's for."

Marcy is adept at using her creative right hemisphere, but she has let her practical left hemisphere get rusty. She's afraid she can't use the skills provided by the left hemisphere, which like any skill will need development if it has lain fallow for too long. This type of thinking needs stimulating.

The right side of the brain is creative and artistic. It is from this side of the brain that spacial orientation is learned. This side of the brain is adept in coining metaphors and similes, and putting these on paper, on canvas, in notes, or in life. The left hemisphere is practical. It deals with numbers, straight lines, and ordered sequences. Most people have a one-sided development partially because of cultural influences and preferences and partially because it's simply easier to be lopsided. The lucky person uses both sides of his brain. He or she is inventive and practical at the same time, and he or she has worked hard to develop full brain power.

Which side of your brain is rusty? In order to have full brain power, you're going to have to oil and move the rusty cells.

Practitioners of Yoga have been using relaxation techniques for centuries, and recently biofeedback methods have demonstrated how these techniques operate. Relaxation is necessary for the development and the use of the right hemisphere. So if you have a rusty right hemisphere, the following exercises will help oil and free those rust-frozen cells.

• Total Body Relaxation: In Yoga, this is known

as the Sponge. When you first begin to practice this technique, lie in a prone position. As you become proficient, you can relax in any position.

Breath control is the first step. Until breath control becomes automatic, place your right hand on your left shoulder. Later, you'll be able to let both arms lie limply on the floor.

When breathing, your diaphragm is going to do the work. Imagine a string tied to your diaphragm that is pulled down as you inhale and slowly let go when you exhale. Your abdomen will rise on inhalation and fall on exhalation if you're breathing correctly. Your arm will remain almost still. Breathe on a slow count in the following manner:

Inhale—1, 2, 3, 4
Hold—1, 2
Exhale—1, 2, 3, 4
Hold—1, 2

Once you've mastered the deep-breathing technique, you're ready to move to the next step—neutral thinking or mind blanking.

To do this, you're going to have to give up control of your thoughts. Practitioners of Yoga often use a set word or tone, such as "Om." You can also use a phrase like "I don't care—I won't try." Repeat your word, tone, or phrase for five to ten minutes.

At first, you'll be able to achieve mental relaxation, but then a random thought of body sensation like an itch will take over. When this happens, don't get upset or excited and lose your rhythm. Simply resume deep breathing and concentrate on your chosen phrase.

From here, it's time to move into total body relaxation. Start from your head and move down to your toes. Begin with your scalp and forehead muscles. Tense them and hold this tension while you count to four. Then relax. Do this with all your muscles. Once you have achieved total body relaxation, you'll find the next session easier. Think of yourself as a sponge lying in the sun soaking up heat. You'll feel loose, heavy, and hot.

• Brainstorming is another method of stretching your creative right brain. I once overheard a group of people doing this for fun, but brainstorming can also be employed seriously. This group of people planned a whole religion based on consumerism. While they were having fun, they developed a number of interesting concepts. They composed hymns and creeds, planned religious centers, and set up a hierarchy.

Practitioners of Yoga use a similar technique. They meditate on a single word, such as "camel." The mind is allowed to free-associate, letting any idea come into the mind. Poets also do this. Look at this line: "Your voice—a whisper out of yesterday—raises the hairs of my mind." The poet was talking about what happened in her memory, but the image used is unique and was derived from allowing her mind to range free.

Now, try this exercise. You are trying to select a gift for a good friend. Money is no object, but you want this gift to be a special offering. Jot down as many things as you can think of, always keeping your friend in mind.

Think of things from diamond rings and sports cars to the gift of a day at a special place you know—perhaps a picnic where you can almost touch the clouds.

Brainstorming can be used to stimulate ideas. With practice, you'll discover many ways to use this method of unlocking creative thinking.

• Another way of stimulating right-brain activity is by stretching your verbal creativity. Take a word such as "confrontation" or "Thanksgiving" and see how many words you can make from these letters in three minutes. If you can find more than twenty, your verbal creativity is well honed.

• Take a simple sentence such as "The ham sandwich tastes good," or "Mary looked sad." Create a picture by adding adjectives o. changing words. "This moldy ham sandwich is good for nothing." "Mary looked as though the tears in her eyes would spill down her face any minute." Once you've been able to create a sentence picture, use the starting sentence to create a paragraph.

When you were a child in school, your left brain was exercised regularly. When you memorized dates and events, as well as poems, learned to solve mathematical problems, and looked at logical progressions, this is what you were doing. Crossword puzzles and "brain teasers" are also excellent exercises for the left brain. If you've set aside your practical left brain for the use of the creative right, buy yourself a book of puzzles and work on them. There are also other exercises you can do:

- Select a poem you like and memorize it.

- Practice categorizing items. One way to do this is to play "Alphabets." Take a category, perhaps authors, animals, or one that's of special interest to your field. In my case, medicines could be used. Try to list a specific for each letter of the alphabet.

  A—Aspirin
  B—Bacitracin
  C—Coumadin (and so forth).

- Try to compound the interest on your savings account, or do complex mathematical problems in your head.

- When you read an article in a magazine or a newspaper, after you are finished, try to write down the important facts. Remember the newspaper reporter's list of questions: "Why?" "Who?" "What?" "When?" "Where?" "How?"

A number of years ago, cars were getting longer and more ornate. There seemed to be status acquired in this country by being the owner of a car that was bigger, faster, and more posh than your neighbor's. Then along came the VW Beetle, a car that was just the opposite of the trend. Suddenly, the roads were full of those tiny buglike vehicles that were contrary to the ordinary trend.

This is just one example of contrary thinking. Contrary thinking involves finding a new use for an old item: Make that empty wine bottle into a lamp. It also involves looking at the trends and coming up with something that heads in the opposite direction. Fashion designers are skilled in this type of thinking. The following exercises will help you stretch your contrary-thinking powers:

- New uses for old items is one way of developing contrary thinking. For each of the following, try to think of as many ways to use them as possible. Try to avoid using the obvious like using bricks to build things:

    Bricks, safety pin, knitting needle, candle, chewing gum, bed sheet, postage stamps, bottles, bottle caps.

- Select a problem you're trying to solve, or any skill you have that may be turned into an opportunity. Perhaps you're having difficulty in your marriage. It could be that you're a marvelous letter writer.

Problem	Assumption	Solution
My husband (wife) doesn't pay enough attention to me.	He or she is too tired from work to pay attention to me.	Learn how to make him pay attention to me in spite of his tiredness.

Contrary solution: Give him or her a quiet time with the newspaper and a drink before I intrude by asking for attention. Or when he or she comes home tired, offer a back rub.

Skill	Assumption	Opportunity
Letter writing	People like to read letters I write.	Writing novels

Contrary thinking: Set myself up as someone who will write letters of complaint for others.

Patterns of thinking and types of thought are important for seeing possible opportunities. Many people find opportunities, but their luck doesn't allow them to realize them. Is it luck, or is it their reaction to taking chances? How do you react to risks?

Out on a Limb

Limb sitting is a learned skill, but if you're going to realize your opportunities and become lucky, you're going to have to learn how it's done. You may look at someone who takes what you consider to be risks and think, "How lucky he (or she) is." If you ask this person why the risk was taken, the person may not understand why you consider what was done as a risk. The person was sure of what he (or she) was doing. Attitude has a lot to do with determining if something is a risk or not.

Peter and Paul were psychiatric residents at the same time and in the same program. During the residency years, Peter shone, but it's Paul who's the success today. During their residency, Peter took the safe course and was the star pupil because he came up with the expected answers and followed the accepted treatment programs with the patients. He was never wrong, according to the standards set by his professors. Paul often tried new techniques, and there were times when he climbed so far out on a limb that it snapped under his weight. Then he took a tumble. But he dusted himself off and climbed back up. After they finished their residency, Peter found a safe niche in a state hospital system. He's now trying to live the way people think a doctor should live, on a salary of $40,000 a year. Paul again climbed out on a limb and set up a practice. He nearly starved the first two years, but now he's living as people think a doctor should live, on $150,000 a year.

Here we see two men who had the same training, but who reacted in different ways to risk-taking. In some ways, they epitomize the two ways of reacting to stress caused by taking risks. Peter is flight and Paul is fight. If you look closer and find the two extremes on the scale, you see that Peter didn't really choose flight; he's really in retreat. Paul, on the other hand, has stopped being a Branch Breaker and has learned to control his reactions to risk. He has become a Limb Sitter.

These two responses must be kept in balance for you to be able to respond to opportunities. Stress often results from the rapid accumulation of decision-needing situations in your life. It's natural either to run or to come out with both fists flailing. But it doesn't have to be that way. To avoid sending yourself into one of these two panic states, there are three important steps to take when dealing with stress caused by an opportunity that calls for a decision:

• Reduce the number of decisions to be made.

• Reduce the time pressure.

• Increase your coping skills.

When Susan arrived at my office, she was clearly in a panic state, and she couldn't decide which way she wanted to act: fight or flight. She appeared to be running in circles while standing still. "I don't know what to do," she said. "It's March, and last year I set June as a time for a separation from Bob. I thought I could clear up the debts by then and be self-supporting. That inheritance I got from my aunt didn't really help. It's all gone, and there are still debts, and the boys' tuition to put in the bank. I need six thousand dollars by August. Then there's my career. It's nowhere. I have skills in two different fields and I can't seem to find a job in either. All I seem to do is sit and cry one minute and run wild the next. I don't even seem capable of killing myself."

Susan was definitely reacting to a number of stress-producing opportunities and decisions: marital problems, financial difficulties, career decisions, and child-related problems. In order to take advantage of the opportunities she would have, she was going to have to reduce the number of decisions she had to make, reduce the time pressure, and increase her coping skills.

The first step for Susan was to set priorities. Priorities depend on need and time. Once priorities have been set, they should be followed, one step at a time, efficiently and easily. Let's see how Susan set her priorities.

- To make a job decision and to re-examine opportunities in this area.

- To explore alternate methods of obtaining tuition for her sons.

- To reduce the debt load.

- To get a separation from Bob.

Once Susan set her priorities, she saw that the deadlines she had set needed to be changed. She found that she didn't need to have the full year's money in the bank before the semester began, and she saw that the June deadline for the separation was putting her under unneeded pressure. She was able to apply the seven thinking methods and the six winning strategies toward career opportunities and toward success.

When I saw Susan a year after she finished therapy, she was a changed person. "I'm lucky," she said, "and I'm working hard to see that I stay that way. I've finally learned to take risks without running scared."

Four general types of reactions to crawling out on a limb can be identified. You can probably place yourself in one of these classes. They are: Nonclimber, Trunk Clutcher, Branch Breaker, and Limb Sitter. Three of these classes haven't learned how to deal with opportunities. Only the Limb Sitter is able to combine flight with fight to achieve planned risk taking. He's the person who can spot an opportunity and take advantage of it to the fullest. The Limb Sitter works hard to become a magnet that draws opportunities. Which one of these risk takers are you?

The Nonclimber faces opportunities with his eyes shut. They don't exist because he can't see them. Deep inside, this person knows that luck is a matter of hard work, and that's what he (or she) doesn't like. The Nonclimber doesn't complain about his luck. He (or she) doesn't envy the lucky person, and it takes a real goad to make him aware of what's going on around him. This person is content to stay at the bottom of the tree.

The Trunk Climber has managed to see an opportunity, but when it comes to cashing in on it, he freezes and holds tightly to his past performances. By freezing, and through a timid approach, he spends a lot of time dreaming about the opportunity he discovered, but he doesn't work to achieve it. You may often hear him echo these words: "I don't have any luck. Things just don't work out for me." He may be so far gone on a fantasy trip that you may hear him say: "Things will work out. I have a lot of faith that when I need something it will appear." The reality is that he hasn't moved from the past in many years. He has a lot of luck, but it's all on paper or in his head.

The Branch Breaker plunges into every opportunity he finds. Sometimes he's engaged into trying to realize three or four different ones at the same time. Every time a new idea comes along, he climbs out and scurries to the thin end of the branch. While he appears to be working hard, he's really scattering his energies. He's often heard to say, "It was a great opportunity, but the public wasn't ready for it. It's hard to get people to accept things that are out of the ordinary. I've just had a run of bad luck." He is enthusiastic, though, and he doesn't let bad luck and poor planning stand in the way of plunging and failing again.

The Limb Sitter finds a place on the limb that will hold him comfortably, and he establishes himself firmly. He neither runs and hides, nor does he plunge into opportunities. He's learned to balance his fight or his flight reactions and he always seems to choose the right action for each opportunity he finds. But then, he works hard.

Mr. (or Ms.) Limb Sitter is always looking for opportunities. When he finds one, he doesn't plunge in after it too soon. First, he analyzes the opportunity by using the seven methods of thinking:

- Broad-scope

- Fine-detail

- Vertical

- Horizontal

- Creative right-brain

- Practical left-brain

- Contrary

By doing all this, he can see all the facets of the opportunity he has found. He may, in the process of exploration, be blessed with serendipity, or a fortunate discovery of other opportunities within the original. Having finished his exploration, he begins to design a pattern of realization by employing the six winning strategies:

- The Rules of the Game

- The Human Factor

- The Compatibility Quotient

- The Rule of Need

- The Law of Supply and Demand

- The Principle of Minimax

Finally, the Limb Sitter looks to himself and discovers ways in which he can sell others on his opportunity. By doing this, he uses the three techniques of image changing, which we'll explore:

- The Rejection Index

- The Appearance Gauge

- The Political Personality

As you can see, the Limb Sitter works hard to use the opportunities he has found. Most people would call him lucky.

CHAPTER

4

Lucky Vibes

The Magnetic Personality

Have you ever noticed how some people seem to draw others to them? There's the man who needed a loan for his potentially successful business or it woud have folded before it got off the ground. He, providentially, found someone who would sponsor him. What about the person in your office who got promoted over everyone's head, and he wasn't the boss's nephew? Or, picture two women with their arms full of packages, facing a closed door. One has the door held open for her, while the other has to contort herself to open the door and to maintain her grasp on her packages. Then, remember that unassuming woman you met at a party the other week. Her husband looked like a Greek god, yet he hovered at her side and treated her like a queen, while your husband ignored you.

57

If looks counted, you would rate higher on the scale than she would. How did these people attract the right attention from others? "They're lucky," you may respond. "If I were lucky, these things would happen to me. I just don't attract other people."

It doesn't have to be that way. What these people have done is to create a lucky aura. No one is born with a lucky aura, but their early years can help create the emotional patterns necessary for the development of this image of themselves. This isn't the entire reason, though. Lucky people don't depend on ease or past performance. They wear their lucky auras like an extra skin, and to keep it fitting perfectly, they exercise it. Think of what happens when you're dieting if you don't exercise. You're left with a skin that doesn't fit. In fact, if you don't exercise regularly, you find yourself out of shape. To maintain your body, you have to exercise; to maintain your lucky aura, you have to exercise it, too.

Politicians exercise their lucky auras, and they don't wait until just before elections, either. They try to wear their aura every day. If they didn't, they wouldn't get elected again and again. Although you may not like politicians, and you may think there's something false about them, you'll have to admit that the successful ones have achieved what they set out to do. They've created an image in which other people want to invest.

A very liberated woman I know has difficulty understanding what women's lib is all about. She's never thought of herself as other than feminine, and she's never failed to be successful in her chosen profession of law. She competes effectively with men. A group of women's libbers confronted her one evening. "You're lucky," they said.

"Luck, my dears, has nothing to do with what I've done," she replied. "I've learned to project an image of confidence and competence better than you have. Fortunately my parents fostered these attitudes, but even if they hadn't, I would have worked to achieve it myself, once I realized this was what the game is all about. It's been hard not to choose the easy way out, and I will admit women are encouraged to do just this. For a number of years, I worked hard to appear fortunate, and others began to notice. Then the breaks began to come. How you appear to others is important if you're going to succeed in life."

Those lucky vibes given off by some people are based on their developed personalities. Personality is developed; you're not born with a set character. "I'm shy," you may say. "I'm not pretty or handsome." "I'm awkward." "I don't know how to react to other people." You don't have to be outgoing, graceful, or beautiful to attract the attention of other people. Look at Abraham Lincoln. He wasn't handsome, but he became a winning politician. Outgoingness, gracefulness, and beauty may initially help you draw other people to you, but these people aren't going to stay if you don't know how to react to people. People aren't going to want to help you if you're only veneer.

How do you react to other people? Do you turn them off, ignore them, or run roughshod over them? Would you want to help someone who treated you in these manners?

Many people know what it is about other people that makes them run away, or they know what attracts them. What they can't do is apply this knowledge to themselves. Have you ever heard someone complain about behavior in other people that they were guilty of themselves? Some people seem deliberately to cultivate traits that cause other people to reject them. This is fine if you want to be a hermit who gleans the woods for his food and clothing. It's not fine if you want other people to notice you in a positive way and to help you when you need a little boost in order to cash in on the opportunities you've found.

The traits you exhibit that drive other people away form your Rejection Index. How high is yours? Take the following quiz to help you calculate it and to see which rejection traits you use in your interactions with others. Respond with "True" or with "False" to each of these questions:

1. When I see someone acting like an ass, I don't hesitate to let him and everyone else know.
2. I like my life to follow comfortable and ordinary patterns with few hassles and changes.
3. I think Archie Bunker's out on a limb.
4. I expect people to "do as the Romans do" when they are in my house.
5. I like to be part of the crowd.
6. My motto is, "Do it the right way—mine."
7. I believe that "a little flattery goes a long way."
8. I think that buying things for someone is a good idea if you want to get your own way.
9. I'm really curious about what makes other people tick.
10. When I see someone crying, I'm glad to lend a handkerchief or a shoulder.
11. I never vote because I know one person can't make a difference.
12. My kids never do anything wrong.
13. I think Betty's (or Tom's) body is better than mine.
14. I really believe I know a lot.
15. I can close my eyes to the things I don't like.
16. Men (or women) are like streetcars; there's bound to be another along any minute.

Now check your answers against the following chart. There are six rejection traits, and the answers given will point to the traits you may have.

- Judgment—1. T; 2. T; 3. F

- Control—4. T; 5. F; 6. T

- Manipulation—7. T; 8. T

- Indifference—9. F; 10. F; 11. T

- Superiority—12. T; 13. F; 14. T

- Avoidance—15. T; 16. T

The Rejection Index looks at your behavior and sees the patterns that cause you to be rejected by others. You may be able to operate on an interpersonal level with one of these traits, but with more, you'll propel people backward rather than drawing them toward you. In this case, you may feel as though you forgot to put on deodorant when you're with people. To help rid yourself of these traits that cause people to run away, you have to become proficient at the game of opposites.

Jim likes to play judge, and his wife has grown tired of it. During the past year, she has stopped going to parties with him on those few occasions when they are invited. "He makes me want to scream," she said. "On the way home, all I hear is, 'John is an alcoholic. Did you see how much he drank tonight?' 'That Susan is a real ballbuster. She leads Joe around by the nose.' I wonder what he says about me behind my back? If he doesn't change soon, I'm going to do something drastic. It worries me because our children are picking up this habit. Jim says I've stopped going out with him, but the truth is that people have stopped asking us out."

Judgment is the process of evaluating others by your standards, which you deem right, and there are no questions about the rightness allowed. Rather than recognizing how other's behavior or attitudes make you feel, you're apt to make a blanket statement. The opposite of judgment is description.

Instead of applying a stereotype or calling names, try stating how you feel and what this person makes you want to do. Instead of saying, "Larry got that promotion because he's an ass kisser," try thinking, "I'm angry because Larry got the promotion because I thought it should have been mine. I think he used methods I couldn't or wouldn't use." Judgment is one way to lose points with others because your listeners aren't sure when they'll end up as victims of your tongue.

When you go to Milton's house, he has the whole evening planned. He doesn't like to be at loose ends, so when he invites you over, there is usually a specific purpose. Milton also doesn't drink. He won't even serve liquor in his house, and he won't go to a restaurant that has a bar. "If you like me, you'll do what I want to do," is the way he feels about life. A lot of people think he's a wet blanket.

A controller wants to do things his way, and he wants to make decisions for those with whom he's involved. A little self-righteousness goes a long way, as people who use this trait may learn. Even parents learn they can't completely control their children's lives and expect them to function as adults. The opposite of control is spontaneity, and if you like to be in control, it may seem hard at first. Practice going along with the crowd and bite your tongue when you want to be boss. Sit back when a problem occurs and see what other solutions people derive. You may learn there is more than one way to do a job. Institute brainstorming sessions. These are excellent for finding alternate solutions and for relinquishing those tight reins. Remember that it's natural for people to resent others wanting to control them. Perhaps this is the reason you jump in and take control before you're controlled.

Susie is quick with a smile and a compliment. "Gee, I like your dress," she says to the office manager. "You've got nice eyes," she says to the new guy at the desk next to hers. She brings flowers from her garden to her boss, but she never gives a gift or a compliment to anyone when it won't benefit her. It doesn't seem worth her efforts to be nice when she won't gain.

If you're a manipulator who thinks flattery and gifts can get you anywhere, you might try honesty. Manipulation may be effective—until other people catch on to how you're pulling their strings. Mothers learn this lesson quickly. The first few bribes will work with a child, but sooner or later, the child either holds out for a bigger reward, or he will disregard the reward and refuse to move. Instead of offering your child a milkshake, tell him why he has to see the doctor or dentist. Rather than bringing your wife flowers and candy so she will arrange a dinner for your boss, explain why this is important to your future and to hers.

"Why should I care how he feels?" said Mary, a nurse, to another nurse. "He asks for pain medication every three hours and I'm usually there on time. I don't understand why he told his doctor I'm a poor nurse. I don't have time to be social. He has nothing but praise for *you*, and a lot of times you're late with his medication."

"I guess it's because I know what pain is like," responded Jean. "I've talked to him about the pain I felt after my car accident. I also have a smile and a few minutes for a joke or a few kind words."

"You can't identify with your patients like that. You'll burn out."

By not caring what the other person thinks or feels, you are practicing indifference. Empathy or putting yourself in the other person's place is the opposite of this trait. Begin by watching other people. Then take the time to learn what is happening in their life. Think about your own past and see if you can discover a similar situation. Try to remember how you thought or felt at that time. Finally, imagine what you would do if you were in his place.

"My father can beat up your father," yelled Joey. "My bike is better than yours." "My grades are better than yours." Joey has grown up now, but he still retains this habit, though his manner of expression has changed. "You should see my Porsche. It's too expensive to drive to work, though." "I met this sensational girl last week. She couldn't keep her hands off me."

Superiority is being sure that you, your possessions, or your achievements are better than those of others. It's also letting others know what you think whether by direct or by subtle means. If you're guilty of this rejection trait, you can shift into reverse by using equality. Just keep reminding yourself that you are equal to other people, and stop worrying about being less. This fear is often the cause of someone assuming superior attitudes. If you really think you are superior, hold back on putting the fact before everyone. Try thinking that other people also have superior qualities even though they may not be the same as yours.

Tracy is forty, unattached, and lonely, though she won't admit this. She's overweight, but she makes no move to go on a diet. "I'm always busy," she says. "I never think about marriage. It's not for me. It means giving up too much. A woman has to do that, and she usually gets a raw deal. I read a lot, go to movies, and watch television. That's enough for me."

Avoidance stems from a fear of getting involved. Although you may pretend something you don't like doesn't exist, the other fellow won't. This rejection trait is one that will keep you from the marriage altar and from a full participation in life. The opposite of avoidance is involvement. Try taking some classes, or finding things that take you out of your shell and into the company of other people. Keep your eyes open, and when you see things you don't like, find a forum, like writing a letter to the editor.

The first step in creating a lucky aura that gives off lucky vibes is to study yourself and see what you're doing that turns other people away. After you've done this, play the game of opposites. Before you know it, you'll be aware of other people, and this change in attitude will help you see them differently.

The reverse is also true. Then you'll be able to move to the next level of becoming a magnetic personality.

For Appearance Sake

When you're trying to attract the attention and help of other people, your whole appearance counts. Which of these people would you rather trust yourself or your money to?

- Joe isn't handsome, but he keeps himself in shape and he walks with his head erect and his back straight. He smiles when he notices other people are watching him. When he talks to someone, his glance meets theirs. He dresses neatly and with an individual air without being flamboyant.

- Larry could have a pleasant face, but he wears a perpetual frown. He walks with his head and shoulders bent. You can pass him on the street, but unless you directly confront him, he'll never know you're there, and he closes his eyes when he talks to you. Although his clothes are expensive and right in style, they never seem to fit him properly, nor do they seem to be in fashion when he's wearing them.

Is Joe your choice? He is for most people. Although Larry may have much to offer, people aren't going to see his good qualities. His appearance from head to toe repels rather than draws. Are you guilty of this? One way of casting lucky vibes is by making sure your appearance counts in the eyes of others.

Begin by putting your best face forward. You may not be a Greek god or goddess, but you can make the best of what you have. Watch your face in a mirror. How does your face appear when you're going to a party or when you have just received a bit of good news? How does it appear when you have to do something that is distasteful or boring? Quite a difference, isn't there?

Now that you've identified your confidence face, practice it in a mirror at home. This may send you into gales of laughter because it's hard to force your features into paths they aren't used to, but it's necessary. To help, try pretending. Recall the last time you had good news or were excited about a party or a trip.

Once you've mastered the face change in the mirror, you'll have to take it out into the world and show it to others. I overheard two women, who had returned to nursing after twenty years at home, talking. "I'm petrified," said one. "I'm sure it shows. How can you look so confident and relaxed?"

"It's a fake," said the other woman. "I don't feel that way inside. Actually, instead of thinking about the hospital and sick people, I'm thinking about the party I'm going to next week. It's called diversion thinking, and when I feel my facial muscles tightening, I think, 'Party, party.' "

Poor posture projects a defeated body image, especially if you creep around with your shoulders bent. If you want to appear more confident than you really are, keep your head erect. The only time you need to watch your feet is when you're climbing over rough terrain and you're in danger of making a misstep that will cause an accident. Your feet don't need close attention. They're capable of functioning on their own quite well.

Once you lift your head and straighten your back, your body image will change in the eyes of others. There's more to body image than posture, though. Make a list of the lucky people you know. Then turn the pages of magazines and look for pictures of those people whom other people term lucky. Did you notice that these people are in control of their bodies, and not the other way around? Have you noticed that not many of these people were grossly overweight or skeletal in appearance? By being in control of their bodies, they project confidence. And confidence attracts the attention and good will of others.

I watched this happen with Barbara, a writer I know. When I first met her, she was overweight and out of shape. She was working as a ghostwriter, and she had difficulty getting commissions, though she was good. One day, she took herself in hand and began to take control of her body. Her confidence has grown with every pound she has shed and every inch she has lost. "It's all a state of mind," she said. "Before when I met a prospective client for a book, I *shlumped* because I felt awkward and lumpy. Now that I'm looking better, I'm able to sell myself to these people. They're willing to look at my writing abilities. All of a sudden, people are telling me I'm getting lucky breaks. If they only knew how hard I've worked. I'm getting ready to do a book on my own, and if it sells, I'll have to sell myself to the public."

"How are you going to do that?" I asked.

"Continue with my losing streak as far as weight goes, and also I'm going to pay more attention to the way I dress."

There have been books written on how to dress so you can appear successful in all the areas of life. Some companies even hire consultants to show their executives how to dress properly for business success and for inspiring confidence in others. Your lucky vibes are based on your ability to inspire this confidence. Attire may have a great deal to do with your luck in business, romance, and in life in general, particularly when you're standing on the bottom rung. Once the world is aware you're a lucky person, you may not need the same aids to bring you to the attention of other people. You may be able to stop smiling and wear rags, but not when you're climbing. During this period of your life, the right clothes for each occasion may help evoke your lucky aura.

Tammy wanted to be promoted to the job of office manager, which she knew would be opening in six months. She had been rather casual about her dress while she was a member of the office secretarial pool. Suddenly she discarded her jeans and baggy pants, the dramatic blouses and sweaters and her very fashionable platform shoes. She started wearing suits and dresses, and her changed appearance brought her to the attention of the higher-ups. They soon not only noticed her change in attire, but they also began to see her abilities, and the job was hers.

Ray figuratively fell on his face at a ski resort one weekend. He's generally found that he's had the pick of the women when he's out. On Friday night, he arrived at the resort late and went to the lounge without bothering to change from his suit and tie. "It was a bust," he said. "I felt out of place, and the faces of the girls said I didn't belong. I rushed upstairs and changed into jeans and a sweater. What a change that made!"

Your face, your posture, your body image, and your clothes unite to form the image you project. You can project failure or success. The person who is lucky projects an image of success. Politicians are adept at projecting images, and that's because they've learned how to cultivate a particular frame of mind.

The Political Personality

Politicians have developed a knack for sending out lucky vibes. Some are said to have charisma, while others don't, yet they also succeed. But charisma radiating or not, the successful politicians have learned how to project an image. While you may not want to be an office holder, you can learn to project your own political personality that tells others you're a winner.

The name of the game is winning when you set out to project an image. The first step you must take is to define the image you want to project. Is your choice a flamboyant personality, an electrical sensation, or is it the quiet restfulness of confidence? Much may depend on the area where you're striving for success. You will want to project one image if you're looking for monetary backers; another if you're seeking romance; a third if you're looking for a promotion at work; and still another if you want to be lucky in marriage. In fact, to have a full and lucky life, you'll need to be able to make frequent and quick changes in the image you project.

A young man of my acquaintance just won a big promotion by his ability to change images in the middle of an interview with his boss. "I went in there wearing my rising-young-executive mask," he said. "I couldn't see why it wasn't working. It's been successful with clients and middle-management people, but my boss was ignoring it. I stopped and listened to what he was saying. Then I brought out the image I'd used in college with a lot of success, that of a bright student eager to learn from the master. It worked and the job was mine." He laughed. "That's how I got Rose to accept my proposal. When I went from eager young lover to dauntless protector, she said 'Yes.' It works with my kids, too. I'm usually loving, playful Daddy, but a shift in image to loving, stern father will bring them under control."

Your words will play an effect on the image you choose to create. Often the tone of your voice will say more than you intend. If you've ever trained a dog, you will understand how this works. You can say anything to a dog if you keep your voice friendly and he'll listen. When you're saying "No" to anyone, there has to be some force behind your refusal. A soft, slurred "No" may be taken by your audience to mean "Maybe." Have you ever overheard a quarrel in which one of the parties agreed by screaming "YES!"? Do you really think he (or she) meant that "Yes!"? Contrast that response with a "Yes" that sings with happiness.

One morning, I overheard my daughter, who was nearly

two, talking to herself. She was repeating the word "No" using different tones of voice and different inflections. What fascinated me was the way I interpreted her different versions of the word "No." I learned something about voice tone that day that I've tried to remember when I'm relating to others.

The words you choose may be important in creating the image of yourself as a winner. Compare these two statements:

- I'm sure you'll want to buy this impressive artifact.

- You wouldn't want to buy this old thing, would you?

While these are perhaps extremes of expression, the first statement will attract your interest and curiosity, while the second will permit you to slam the door in the salesman's face. If you're guilty of door-slamming speech when you're trying to sell yourself, no one's going to buy. Many people aren't aware they use these patterns, and they put their lack of self-salesmanship down to bad luck.

Learn to listen to yourself when you talk to other people. If you have a tape recorder, record some conversations when you're trying to be persuasive, and when you play the tape back, listen to yourself. After you get over the shock of hearing your own voice, you can begin to discover the way you slam the door on yourself through your choice of words. After you've analyzed your choice of words, take the same things you said and turn them into winning speeches. Then practice encounters with others before you have them. You may sound stilted for a while, but one day you'll discover that self-salesmanship has become natural for you.

Poor grammar and pronunciation of words can also close your listener's ears. You can have the best ideas in the world—ones that are sure money-makers—only to have people ignore you because they think you're illiterate or that you're showing off. In a heated discussion, slips and lapses of speech will go unnoticed, but you've got to capture people's attention first. This doesn't mean you can't use new words, but look them up in the dictionary first. Learn not only how to say these words, but also learn what they mean. It could spare you embarrassment from using the wrong word at the wrong time. It will also keep your audience from falling asleep because they don't know the meaning of your words, especially if you're using jargon. Professionals—doctors and lawyers—are often guilty of this.

Once when I was a medical student, I remember a time when I made both errors in the same sentence. As a medical student I was learning a whole new vocabulary, and through this, I caused the conversation at a party to come to a halt. One of my friends walked into the room sporting a cast on his left leg. "Was it a tibula or a fibia?" I called. The nonmedical people thought I was talking about a new kind of ski, but my medical friends knew I should have said "tibia" and "fibula."

If you want to create a winning image, stop before you speak. Think about your tone of voice, avoid door slammers, and watch your grammar, pronunciation, and the meaning of your words. These cautions will help you create the image that suits you best in each new or old situation.

Putting Your Lucky Aura Together

You may not be able to synthesize your winning image overnight. A building that's put together in a slapdash fashion has no endurance. You aren't planning to acquire your lucky aura as a one-shot deal. I'm sure you want others to have this view of you forever, and for something to last, careful planning and hard work are needed.

A patient of mine, Julie, had to build a new image of herself after a divorce that occurred when she was thirty-six. She had quit school to marry Joe, and had thrown herself into the marriage and motherhood. During her married years, she lost her previous image of herself as a bright student who was ambitious. She did work hard to help Joe succeed. And he did, but Julie acquired an image of herself as a dull housewife. She sold this image to everyone. Joe began to believe it, and he found himself a younger, more alive woman.

When I first met Julie, my thoughts were, "She could be attractive, but she's not." Her clothes looked like they belonged to an older woman, and she didn't smile. Her whole body image was one of indifference and avoidance. I pointed this out to her, and sent her home to begin practicing the opposites of these two traits: empathy and involvement.

Slowy, a different Julie began to emerge. Then we moved to phase two of her development. Julie was encouraged to look at herself from head to toe. She invested in a diet program and some ballet lessons. The diet program improved her figure, and the ballet lessons helped her gain control of her body. She began to move differently.

Julie's life then began to change rapidly as her appearance changed. On her own, she began to improve her verbal skills. She found phase three of creating a winning image on her own.

A year after her divorce, Julie met a man, but he didn't ask her to marry him. That wasn't what was on his mind, nor was it on his mind to give her a job, but he did.

"I shifted images on him," said Julie. "I saw he wasn't serious about our relationship becoming something permanent. I do like what the second image got me—an exciting career in public relations. It gives me independence. Remember when I had that 'You wouldn't want to hire me, would you?' attitude? I'm pushing myself hard at work, and I'm going to school, too." She grinned. "I saw Joe the other day when he came to pick up the kids. He did a double take and then tried to push me back into my old image. I didn't go and I won't go back. Life is too much fun these days."

There are three phases for developing those lucky vibes that attract people to your side:

- Phase one consists of discovering your Rejection Index. Once you've done that, you'll have to identify the rejection traits you use and put the game of opposites into play.

- Phase two involves your appearance. You should practice putting your best face forward. Then you need to gain control of your body and your body image. And finally, you'll discover "Clothes do make the man, and the woman as well."

- Phase three calls for the development of your Political Personality. First, define your present image. Then work to create a new one. After this, you'll learn to change your image as the need arises. Along with creating an image of yourself goes your ability to communicate. You'll need to watch your tone of voice, your choice of words, and your grammar and pronunciation.

By fully developing these three phases, you'll begin to attract attention. One day, to your surprise, you'll find others want to help you win success. "Isn't he [or she] the lucky one," they will say. "I want to be where the luck is."

5

Business Luck

Business Luck

All businesspeople say they work hard to achieve, but often other people who observe them feel this is not the case. These other people think people succeed in the business world by being lucky.

- John won big playing the stock market. "He sure knew how to pick them," other people say.

- Susan made a killing in real estate. "She must have had an inside track to be able to pick and choose so well," is the remark that is made.

- Cindy got a two-step promotion at work. "She was lucky enough to be in the right place at the right time," is the consensus.

- Roger started his own business and now he's seeing it thrive. "Everything he touches turns to gold," is what other people think.

These four people have something in common: They have business luck. But their success required more than luck or mere competence. A little luck never hurts when you're playing the stock market, buying property, or taking your future in hand and seeking a promotion or starting a new business. But how do some people manage to keep winning most of the time, while others, equally competent, fail miserably? Business luck can be acquired. It takes a certain way of thinking to see and grab lucrative business opportunities. When you acquire this skill, others will say, "He's always in the right place at the right time. He sure knows how to pick them. I wonder how he found the inside track. Everything he touches works. He's so lucky."

Winning in the Stock Market

I once heard an elderly woman describe the stock market as a place where you bought pieces of paper instead of groceries. While her idea is simplified, she may be on the right track for a beginner. "I don't buy stocks myself," she said. "I let my broker do that. He's good." This woman uses a strategy that allows her to win, and when she loses, she has someone other than herself to blame. But she has no control over what happens to her money, and she doesn't try to learn. She's a passive investor and looks on her stocks as just a different kind of savings account.

One afternoon, during a conversation with a highly successful stockbroker, I was told that there are two kinds of stocks:

- Long-range investments
- Trading stocks

"How do you know the difference?" I asked.

"Trading stocks are those that must be watched carefully. They demand quick and large acquisitions or sales based on small movements of the market. Long-range investments are stocks that show a small, steady growth. Buying stocks requires you to decide on an investment strategy and stick to it. A lot of my customers are confused about which way to jump."

"You mean you don't tell them which stocks to buy?" I asked.

"I'm an adviser," he said. "You should know how people tend to react to advice. As a doctor, you give people advice about their health, but that doesn't mean they're going to listen. Or maybe they listen only part of the time."

I nodded. "What makes one of your clients a winner on the stock market?"

"One important factor is for them to recognize and consider their personalities. There are two types of winners: the single-shot and the double-barrel.

"The single-shot player on the stock market may be either a trader or an investor. The trader doesn't buy stocks that appreciate gradually. Nor does the investor select stocks that call for quick action.

"The double-barrel player selects his stocks by buying in both categories—long-term and trading stocks. He'll hold onto investment stocks for years, and buy and sell his trading stocks in rapid fashion. He's always sure which stock fits which category."

"How many types of losers are there?" I asked.

"One," he replied. "They are the people who don't know what they're doing. They'll sell any stock when it drops, even though there's a good long-term forecast for it. Or they'll have a favorite stock that they'll cling to until it bottoms and they're left with a piece of paper that is valueless. They just won't listen to advice."

And listening to advice is one of the most important steps in being lucky in any particular field. Most of us have some degree of expertise in some field, but few of us are experts at everything, and this includes the stock market. It makes sense to seek an expert—in this case, a stockbroker. If you want to know about your health, you'll check with a doctor. He's been trained to assess this area of your life. A stockbroker has been trained to assess stocks and the stock market, and his advice will be invaluable. After all, if he's wrong too many times, he won't be able to make a living.

When seeking an expert, the phases mentioned in Chapter 4, "Lucky Vibes," should be followed. What is your Rejection Index when it comes to listening to advice from others? Your track record in this area can easily be determined because you've had occasion in the past to listen to the experts and accept or reject their advice. You've been to doctors; had occasion to consult lawyers; listened to real-estate agents; studied with teachers; and been taught by your parents. What is your track record?

Murray inherited fifty thousand dollars from his uncle and decided to invest it in stocks. He was a teacher, and until now, he had never had any involvement with the stock market. The sudden influx of money went to his head, and Murray followed a pattern of behavior that he had often chosen in the past. Murray became an instant expert by reading a book about the stock market. He studied the reports in his newspaper, selected his stocks, and went to a broker. The broker gave him advice about his chosen stocks, but Murray employed his rejection traits. In six months, he had parlayed his fifty thousand dollars into twenty-five thousand dollars. Then Murray woke up. He identified his rejection traits and played the game of opposites. He also had to find another broker. With this man, instead of his pseudo-expert image, Murray chose the image of student, another past successful image of himself. By doing this, his fortunes changed and he was soon on a winning streak.

After you've mastered your rejection traits and have created your image, you may find you're still not making money from your ventures onto Wall Street. Your frame of mind may be holding you back. Your attitudes may be frozen somewhere between the creative and the practical. Or you could be in the state of flux that the losing stock-market player finds himself in.

To increase your chances of success, you have to look at your patterns of thinking. Where do you stand on the limb? Are you a Nonclimber, a Branch Breaker, a Trunk Clutcher, or a Limb Sitter? Everyone wants to be a Limb Sitter because this is the person who sees an opportunity and goes after it, or many times, the opportunity comes to him. To be a Limb Sitter, you have to apply the seven thought patterns to your problems: broad-scope, fine-detail, vertical, horizontal, right-hemisphere, left-hemisphere, and contrary thinking.

Rose wasn't rich, but she did have a little money to invest in the stock market. She had always been fascinated by this form of investment, but she knew her knowledge was limited to a very broad picture of what the stock market involved. A friend of hers, Don, was a stockbroker, and Rose often asked him questions. One day, he offered to be her mentor. Rose jumped at the chance to learn from an expert.

Through Don, she learned about the fine details involved in trading on the stock market. Rose began to get her feet wet by cautiously investing in obvious growth stocks. Here, she used vertical thinking. One day, she began to think about the periphery of the stock market. She liked what she was doing, but it wasn't enough. Rose decided to become a stockbroker, and her husband encouraged her. She enrolled in college with business and math as her majors. Horizontal thinking had shown her a way to change her life.

In college, Rose found to her dismay that her left hemisphere was rusty. She had been using her right hemisphere for the past ten years almost exclusively. Math was suddenly a drag, but she eased herself slowly into these courses, and her full functioning returned.

When she finished college, Don gave her a job in his office. For nearly a year, Rose walked a conventional course as a stockbroker, until the day she began to apply contrary thinking to her situation. Instead of waiting for clients to come to her, she began to create business among housewives. This had once been her primary life role and she felt these women would relish the chance to make their money work for them. Rose is now earning more than she ever dreamed she would, and her life has taken on a fullness she hadn't thought possible. All she did was change her thinking patterns and employ them to the fullest.

Perhaps you're a person "who knows other people," and are a person who has always used high gear in your thinking processes as you work. How can you create a pattern of success for yourself in the stock market? After all, your success has been derived in a different field and you don't want to spoil your luck by failure here. By employing the six winning strategies, you too can be successful in the stock market.

Roger is a successful lawyer, and he's got a record of success when he plays the stock market. When he began to invest in stocks, the first thing he did was to check his Compatibility Quotient with the idea of investing money in stocks. He knew he had an affinity for mathematics and he was able to think of money as an abstract idea. After determining his Compatibility Quotient, he looked at the Human Factor—himself. He discovered that his temperament would allow him to be a single-shot investor who would invest in growth stocks.

The Rule of Need influenced his decision about the kind of stocks he would buy. He was too busy with the practice of law to keep up with the momentary fluctuations that would call for quick decisions if he bought trading stocks. His immediate needs were taken care of by his thriving law practice, and he was more interested in the long-range benefits of investing. Before he put his money on the line, Roger learned the Rules of the Game. By questioning and reading, he began to understand the language of the stock exchange. Once he did, he turned to the Principle of Minimax and sought a stockbroker who, in the opinion of a number of people, had the best track record. Together, Roger and his broker studied the Law of Supply and Demand as it applied to Roger. Now Roger has a valuable portfolio, and many people think he's a "lucky devil" when it comes to investments. But as you see, it wasn't luck. Roger worked hard so people would think he was lucky at playing the stock market.

Making a Killing in Real Estate

I was talking to a fellow doctor the other day, and my great admiration of his real-estate expertise plainly showed. "How do you know where and when to invest in real estate?" I asked.

"You have to be observant and to know your market," he said. "Here's a quick question for you: What's the fastest growth area in this country?"

A number of answers popped into my head, but I hesitated about committing myself. "I don't know."

"It's Houston, and that's already old news," said Bob. "If you couldn't answer that question, you'd better not invest in real estate."

Though I had an inkling he was right, my face fell. "Why not?"

"It means you're not in tune with what's happening in growth areas, and that's important. Of course, most people aren't going to plunge immediately into real estate on a national scale. They're going to start close to home, and it's easier to learn what's happening locally than it is on a national or an international scale. A lot of big money-makers in real estate are global thinkers. Real estate, by the way, isn't a quick money-maker. If that's why you're investing, find something else. You have to look at real estate as a long-term investment, and it shouldn't be looked on as part of your income-making ventures. I know a lot of people who are making money dealing in property, but they support themselves in other ways."

"How do you get started?" I asked.

"Find yourself a couple of good real-estate agents. Three is a good number. Once you become a preferred customer, you will acquire leverage. This means you can get a mortgage. Brokers like preferred customers, and they will soon learn what kind of property you like."

"Find yourself an expert," I said. "Good advice for anything that is new to you."

"And you have to be careful about who you think the expert is. A lawyer can set up your contracts, and an accountant can look at the books, but don't take their advice on what to buy. Listen to your broker and learn to make your own decisions."

As we talked, I began to see a pattern developing in Bob's techniques for success in the field of real estate. Though he didn't identify his strategies as such, Bob used the six winning strategies with an assist from the other luck-producing techniques.

Compatibility with real estate was very much a part of his advice. He not only advised a compatibility with the field in general, but he said that most people have an affinity for a particular type of real estate. "Some people are into apartment buildings," he said. "Others only invest in office buildings." Still other people buy undeveloped land, and that takes a special kind of insight and imagination. The best approach is to find what's best for you. Then you've got to know your market. It takes a lot of study and research."

Learning the Rules of the Game is vital to success in real estate, just as it is in other life situations. Justice may be blind, but if Lady Luck were painted, she would have both her eyes open. The more knowledge you have, the better you'll be able to make an informed and realistic decision.

The Rule of Need comes into play in the real-estate investment. "Don't be afraid to buy property if it meets your needs, no matter what other people say," advised Bob.

"I thought you were supposed to listen to the experts," I countered.

"You are, but after all, they recommended this property to you. No, the comments you hear will be from people who question your paying a hundred thousand dollars for a building they wouldn't have gone higher than ninety thousand dollars for. You know your reasons for wanting this particular piece of property, or at least you should. They don't."

In our conversation, I learned how Bob applies the Law of Supply and Demand to his real-estate dealings. Prestige buildings are few, but before you buy a particular piece of property, you're going to want to be sure there is a demand for the type of space you will be offering. "There aren't many buildings around like the Empire State Building."

"Who would want to buy that?" I asked.

"I would," replied Bob. "It has 100 percent occupancy, and a prime location. That's everything a shrewd investor would want."

"Back to what you said before. How can you be sure when you buy a particular building that there is a demand for the kind of space you're offering?"

"Ask to see the seller's books and the leases he has with his tenants. Then take a walk around the neighborhood to see if there is a high or a low rate of occupancy in adjacent buildings. Check with the tenants in the other buildings about their leases, or pretend you are looking for space to rent and see how the rents compare to those in the building you are interested in."

"It sounds like hard work," I said.

"Isn't everything that's worthwhile?" asked Bob. "You can lessen the amount of work and share the risks by going into partnership with one or two other people. You'll all have equal responsibility that way, but when you take a partner, you'd better be sure you can work together."

Here Bob is applying the Principle of Minimax as well as the Human Factor. As you can see, Bob uses all six of the winning strategies when he invests in real estate. This application has made him appear lucky to the person who doesn't use these methods.

The person who invests in plots of land instead of apartment or office buildings should be well versed in the use of the seven patterns of thinking: broad-scope, fine-detail, vertical, horizontal, left-hemisphere, right-hemisphere, and contrary thinking. There is more of a speculative nature to this type of real-estate investment than when buying something that has a set purpose. Patterns of thinking must be exercised to predict what the trends may be.

Bob told me that at one time the purchase of single-family dwellings for resale had been a real money-making proposition, but this has changed. Rising mortgage interest rates, higher property taxes, and escalating costs of heating and electricity have changed this market. But who could have known this was going to happen? A person who used his head and could postulate where the trends were leading.

Lou and Sally got trapped in this type of housing venture. They had bought a small apartment building, renovated it, and sold it for a profit. Next they decided to buy a house and do the same thing. They knew interest rates were going up, but they reasoned that people always needed places to live, and that since it was an election year, mortgage rates would drop. By the time they remodeled, the house they had bought for thirty thousand dollars should have been worth at least forty-five thousand dollars because they had spent fifteen thousand dollars for remodeling. They're asking sixty thousand dollars for the house, but it's been on the market for nearly a year, and they've had no takers. Recently, they've had to make repairs because of damage caused by vandals. Soon this house will reach the point where they will lose money even if they sell it.

Carol doesn't buy real estate; she sells it, and her reputation is rapidly growing. She has a knack for getting listings, and often these are exclusive. Her Rejection Index is low, and she has developed skills for changing her image as her clients change. Recently, she was able to list exclusively four houses in one day. One belonged to an elderly woman, one to a doctor, one to a couple who was being transferred, and one to a local policeman. Let's look at how Carol used her ability to change images as she worked to get these house listings.

Mrs. Green was seventy and unable to live alone any longer. Her daughter had called Carol to tell her about the house. When Carol arrived, Mrs. Green was still in her nightgown and housecoat. She took Carol on a tour of the house.

"Mary thinks I should sell," said Mrs. Green. "It's been my house for fifty years. I don't want a lot of people tramping around and nebbing into my things. I don't want to be bothered by strangers."

Carol assumed her "I'll-take-care-of-everything" image in response to Mrs. Green's obvious need. "I'll handle the sale myself," she said. "In fact, I think I know the right people. They're looking for a family house, and this looks like a perfect one for them."

"We raised four kids here, me and John. Yes, it was a good

family house. . . . Well, I'll let them look at it, but I don't want a lot of strangers prowling around."

"There won't be."

From Mrs. Green's house, Carol went to the Raymonds' house; they were being transferred. "We have to get at least sixty thousand dollars for this house, but it has to be a quick sale," said Mr. Raymond. "We have to be in Illinois in six weeks and there's a house to buy there."

"I don't think there'll be any trouble getting your price," said Carol, "but it might be a good idea if you investigate the possibility of a short-term loan to cover a down payment on the house you have to buy. Closings may take as long as three months. I can help you there, if you'd like."

"I thought we'd sell it within two weeks and then have the money right away."

"I wish it would happen that way. It would make life much easier, but banks have to investigate prospective buyers and the house, as well, before they give a mortage. That's good business sense."

"You're right," said Mr. Raymond. "There's just so much to think about right now."

"I'll help you all I can," said Carol. "If you'd like, I'll help you find a realtor in Illinois and let them know what kind of house you're looking for. This may save you a great deal of time."

"That would be good. Thank you."

Again Carol volunteered a lot of assistance while showing an ability to sensibly plan the financial details that Mr. Raymond was too pressed to deal with. She successfully showed herself as an astute businesswoman (which she was)—and one who was looking out for his best interests.

From the Raymonds' house, Carol went to Dr. Jacobs' house. "I really don't have time to handle this myself," he said. "Otherwise, I wouldn't bother with you. You came highly recommended, but I'm not sure I want to give you an exclusive. Wouldn't it make sense for me to have as many people working on this deal as possible?" He laughed. "My patients are always talking about wanting a second opinion."

Carol smiled. "I'll be glad to give you the names of other realtors, but I think this house will sell itself. It has many practical yet decorative features. If you like, you can give me a time period on the exclusive listing and if I haven't sold the house by the end of that time, it can be opened to other realtors."

"I could try that method, especially since you found the new house for us, but I just don't know."

"Why don't you take a few days to decide? I'll call you on Monday."

On Monday, Dr. Jacobs decided to let Carol have the house listing exclusively for three months. Here, her ability to go along with Dr. Jacobs' hesitancy—to respond with a pliant, rather than a pushy, attitude—earned her the listing.

When Carol left Dr. Jacobs' house, she went to the home of Dan Peters, a local policeman. His house had been on the market as a self-sale for nearly two months. "I've heard you realtors have an in with the banks as far as mortgages go. We lost two buyers because they couldn't get a mortgage." Clearly, he was looking to Carol for someone with a solution, and she took on the role of adviser.

Carol toured the house with the Peters. When she finished, she said, "Part of the difficulty in obtaining a mortgage is that there are some necessary repairs that should be done."

"I don't want to sink any money into a house I'm not going to live in," said Dan.

"In that case, you may have to lower your asking price."

"I've read the papers and I know what we're paying for our new house. This house is worth at least what we're asking."

"People don't want to buy a house that means they'll have to put out money immediately for repairs. I'm not advocating major changes, but the bathroom sink should be replaced and the dining-room ceiling repaired. A few hundred dollars spent could bring a return of a few thousand."

"She makes sense," said Mrs. Peters. "Dan, you know we have to sell this house. Why don't we take her advice?"

"O.K, O.K.," said Dan.

Carol explained her success in this way. "I listen to my prospective clients whether they're buying or selling. I have been rather lucky, though. My satisfied customers often send me people who either want to buy or to sell a house."

What Carol calls luck is based on hard work. Carol has gained proficiency in changing her image to fit her clients. She knows where she is going and how she's going to get there.

Getting a Two-Step Promotion at Work

Recently Richard, one of my patients, came into my office wearing a big grin. "I've just been promoted to temporary manager, and the job will be mine if I can prove myself. That strategy you helped me map out to get noticed was effective, but I'm petrified. I thought I was aiming for a small step forward, not a giant leap."

"What will happen if you bomb?" I asked. "Will you lose your job?"

Richard shook his head. "I'll drop back to assistant manager, the job I was aiming for in the first place. I don't want that to happen, though."

"Assess your risks," I said. "You'll still end up with a promotion, which was your aim, and you'll be able to learn from your mistakes."

Richard was a Trunk Clutcher when I first met him. He was a dynamic salesman, but every time he thought about moving into management, he held tightly to the familiar. His supervisors noticed this, and Richard was passed over for promotion on three previous occasions. In therapy, we worked on creating a new image for him.

First, we tested his Rejection Index and discovered that Richard's was very low. He scored one point, and that in manipulation. As a salesman, he used flattery to help him achieve sales, but he seldom used this technique unless the client was extremely difficult.

Richard's appearance was attractive. He kept himself fit by exercising. I sent him home to practice using the confidence face he used with clients in situations where he would be dealing with administrative decisions. We also changed his style of dress to a more conservative manner—suits rather than sport coats and slacks.

Image projection was the third area where we worked to change Richard's image. We talked about his past and made a list of the successful images he had projected. We then selected the ones that would be most effective in what he wanted his future career direction to be.

This three-phase plan didn't create a new Richard. It helped him make use of his skills and abilities in new ways. When he received his promotion, we knew we had been successful. Richard had received an opportunity to advance in his career. Now he had to show he was capable of developing leadership skills and thinking patterns.

A leader has to be able to see around corners as well as to be able to see the obvious. He needs to be creative and practical at the same time. During our next session, Richard and I talked about the various oppositions in thinking patterns:

- Broad-scope vs. fine-detail

- Horizontal vs. vertical

- Right-hemisphere vs. left-hemisphere

- Contrary vs. ordinary

As we talked, Richard saw that his thinking had been totally of the practical type: fine-detail, vertical, left-hemisphere, and ordinary, and that for some reason he had been afraid of his creative moments. When he left the office, he was going home to begin planning changes in his thinking patterns. Because Richard had entered a management position, it was decided that broad-scope and right-hemisphere thinking were his immediate needs, though horizontal and contrary thinking would also be needed for him to succeed. Richard decided to spend the next week with broad-scope vs. fine-detail exercises.

Only time will tell if Richard will be successful in his double move. If he isn't, he will have learned from this experience, and his next opportunity will find him better equipped for success.

Rapid career advancement has become very important to many women, especially those who have delayed their careers until they have raised their families. A friend of mine, Jennie, is taking a refresher course in nursing. Before she began, she went through a set of mind exercises she had designed to help her attain the proper mind-set. While she was not working as a nurse, she kept up with theory through her journals and read the latest drug information. For a month before the course began, she spent time in active recall of her past experience as a nurse.

Jennie also assessed her abilities to handle crisis situations. On the day the course began, she was able to reconstruct in her mind an image of herself as a competent, caring nurse. She realized there had been many changes in nursing, but most of these changes were not as drastic as people thought. Plasticware was being used instead of glass and metal, and there were a number of new machines. She decided to approach the changes as she experienced them and not let them overwhelm her at the start.

"The level of anxiety in the refresher group the first day was high," she told me. "At first, I thought it might be catching, but

I pulled back. The other refreshers began to call me Ms. Cool because I refused to panic or to rush headlong into action. I'm beginning to think there should be prerefresher courses for all women returning to work. They need to know how to get their anxiety under control. Those relaxation exercises you taught me when we were talking about thinking patterns really helped. By the time the refresher course was over, most of the other women had reached the level I had been at when we began. Sometimes I felt out of place because I was already planning the strategies I would employ to help me succeed when I returned to work. I've reached a point of commitment that the other women haven't."

Commitment is a vital step to take if you're seeking a two-step, or even a single-step promotion. If you don't like or don't care about your job, you won't be able to invest yourself in it. Success in business calls for the investment of your energies as well as your money. If you're an employee who's striving for a promotion, you are your own greatest asset.

The six winning strategies can show you how to invest yourself for your greatest potential success. What is your Compatibility Quotient with the job? Do you like this type of work, and does it use your proven abilities to the fullest extent? Have you proven in the past that this type of a job, or a similar one, is right for you?

Before she entered the nursing refresher course, Jennie looked at her Compatibility Quotient with the job. She knew she had liked nursing before she had her family, and that she had abilities that proved she was competent with the sick. She also knew she had leadership qualities. Most of her experience had been in the past, but she had proven herself then. Within a year after her graduation from nurse's training, she had been promoted to the job of head nurse, while many of her classmates were still working as staff nurses.

By taking the refresher course, Jennie was reviewing the rules of a game she hadn't played in years. Some of the rules had changed since her absence from the field, especially those concerned with responsibility and accountability. By knowing the rules she would be able to create a framework in which to work.

The Human Factor came into play in two ways. First, Jennie asked herself if she could work with ill people who might be irritable and frightened. She knew she had done this successfully in the past. Also she looked at her skills at handling her children who often acted like the ill. Next, she evaluated her abilities to work with others. She looked at her committee and volunteer work since she was married and rated herself as A-1 in both leadership and cooperation.

Jennie knew that her needs would be fulfilled by a return to work. She had reached that point in motherhood where her children were becoming increasingly independent. Thus she was no longer content to remain at home. The extra money would serve the Rule of Need in another way, by helping defray the expenses of college-age youngsters.

The Law of Supply and Demand was operating in her favor. There always seems to be a demand for nurses, if you are experienced, but for some reason the need had increased at the time she began her refresher course. Jennie felt the expansion of nurses into other areas was partly responsible for the increased need for hospital nurses.

When she finished her refresher course, Jennie applied the Principle of Minimax to help her return to the hospital. She began to work on a part-time basis in the hospital where she had taken the course because she knew they would be aware of her need for experience. She chose to return part-time for two reasons: to ease herself back into the field, and to give herself additional time to evaluate her response to nursing. A few months later, she enrolled part-time in a B.S. program, thus increasing her chances for success in nursing. Two years after she entered the refresher course, Jennie had her B.S. in nursing and a big promotion. She's now a supervisor and is returning to school for her master's degree. Her constant reapplication of the six winning strategies has been responsible for her continued success.

Starting Your Own Business and Seeing It Thrive

I am a psychiatrist, and until a few years ago my practice involved helping people deal with the effects of stress in their lives on an individual basis. You may be aware of all the recent research done with stress and its effects on people's lives in all areas, but in particular on their physical and emotional lives. High blood pressure, heart attacks, obesity, alcoholism, drug abuse, and acute emotional storms have all been connected to a person's ability or nonability to deal with the effects of stress. Articles have been written about career burn-out as a result of stress, as well as articles on the break-up of relationships and problems in dealing with children.

While my practice dealt with individuals, I began to see a broader picture to the idea of stress. A pattern had begun to emerge. A number of my patients were executives who were faced with career problems and decisions. They began to refer associates of theirs to me. These men realized stress was a part of their lives, and being able to control their reactions to it was essential to their functioning on a competitive level. Other patients were their wives or children, who were reacting to the presence of a distracted husband or father, or to the trauma caused by a recent move. Horizontal thinking was responsible for my seeing the periphery of the effects of stress on these men.

One evening as I was relaxing at home, a thought struck me. "What if there was a way to teach people to deal with the pressures of corporate life and to lessen the impact of stress on the lives of these people? An individual therapy program may not help all those who need help. It was that evening when the idea for Corporate Stresscontrol Services, Inc., was born. But I couldn't stop with the idea. More planning was called for.

After a number of evenings of thought and jotting down my ideas, I was ready to begin action. The new company would have a teaching rather than a therapeutic base, though individual counseling would be part of the plan. After the idea was well formulated, I sat down and applied the six winning strategies to developing the company.

The Compatibility Quotient would figure on at least two levels of operation. First was my own compatibility with the idea and the method used for dealing with stress. I asked myself if I would be able to move from a one-on-one level of counseling to a group-based situation. The answer was affirmative because I knew I had experience dealing with small groups successfully.

The next level where the Compatibility Quotient would operate would arise when I began to hire associates and employees in this venture. I would have to select people who could work together and work with myself and my ideas. They would have to be able to play by the Rules of the Game.

Since this was a new venture, most of the Rules of the Game had to be created. I did study programs that were set up to take care of physical health, and I obtained some ideas for the practical running of the business from these. "Never promise more than you can expect to reasonably deliver," was the motto I set for the company. This would give the company integrity and also prevent me from trying to run it as a one-man show.

The Rule of Need was an important factor in the development of the promotional material for the company, for if the need for our services couldn't be demonstrated, there could be no business. A list of the effects of stress on production and smooth corporate functioning was set up. Among the problems listed as evidence of stress in a corporation were absenteeism, alcoholism, rapid employee turnover, on-the-job accidents, and drug abuse.

The Human Factor came into play on every level of development of the company. Of course, the very premise was based on human reaction to stress. The relationships of the individual staff members to each other and to the clients were of vital importance. Several times, consideration of the Human Factor has made me rethink my goals.

Finally, the Principle of Minimax was applied when I chose associates in other cities. In essence, they were consultants hired by the company, so they worked on a different basis from the regular employees. I also applied this principle by offering my employees incentives for new ideas for strengthening the company.

To become sure of the success of this new venture, I had to become a Limb Sitter. A chance conversation with a neighbor led me to approach his employer with the package we had designed with success. I also had to call a number of corporations and risk turndowns. By applying such producing techniques, the company has grown and the planned risk-taking has paid off.

To appear lucky in the business field, you're going to have to work hard. Those who are at the top aren't there because of a fluke. They've used the techniques that are available to you, if you want to use them.

6

Lucky in Love

The Romance Game

• He always connects every time we go to a bar.
  I'm just as good-looking and as intelligent, but
  I have no luck at all.

• She's never without a date, and I don't know
  how she does it. I've even tried wearing the
  same kind of clothes, but it didn't help. I'm just
  not lucky with men.

What do these lucky daters have that you don't? It would be
nice if it could be distilled and you could rub it on yourself to
help you achieve instant luck in love. The world is full of advice
for would-be daters, and if you followed all the advice, you
could end up in a whirl. This advice doesn't include the
pseudo-advice you constantly see and hear on television, radio,

or in magazines and newspapers. You may not believe the commercials, but how many of these products have you tried just on the off chance they might work? And you'll never succeed in the dating game if you spend your time at home watching television.

To succeed in the dating game, you have to be where the action is. Whether you're making your first attempt, or going around for the second time, third time, or more times, you're not going to find a man or a woman at home, unless you have brothers or sisters who drag their friends there. Where the action is depends on the kind of person you are. Some people make connections at a bar, and others in church. Some find their dates at school, and others on the ski slopes. It's a matter of finding a place where other people congregate who suit your style. Movies are crowded, but this is parallel mingling—you are sitting beside someone but there is no interaction—so that's not a good solution. Make a list of your interests, and also of those things you might like to try. Then find ways to meet people who share these things with you.

Before you enter the dating game, you'd better look at your Rejection Index. Which of the negative traits are your biggest problems? Play the game of opposites until you've eliminated those traits or gotten them under control.

The next step in winning in the dating game is to check your appearance. What does your posture project? Defeat, confidence, or independence? All of these stances can have an effect on your position at the finish line.

Is your face frozen into place, or does it show everything you think and feel? Either of these projections could lose you points. Honesty is great, but sometimes judgments are made too quickly and they're registered on your face. Practice with your mirror to gain an eager, welcoming face with a natural smile. A natural smile is easy to produce for friends. If you want to gain points in the dating game, you'll have to smile the same way for strangers, too.

If you're honest with yourself, you'll know how your body

compares with those of other men or women. When you play the dating game, you have to compete with others, and if your body doesn't measure up, you may be among the losers. Invest some time and energy in pruning away those flabby spots. Diet to reduce the extra amount of poundage you're carrying into the race. All they do is increase your handicap. Not only can these methods bring you attention from others, but they'll also bring you a longer life to enjoy.

Have you ever seen someone arrive at an outdoor barbecue or a picnic dressed totally wrong? A suit and tie for the man, or an evening dress for the woman. They look out of place, and this often makes them act that way. Very few people have the flair to carry off this wrong-dress scenario without losing face. You don't have to run out and buy a wardrobe designed to fit every occasion, but you can learn to fake it. Women have a little more difficulty with faking, but a good rule to remember is, "Before you buy an article of clothing, check its usefulness."

Soon after Marsha was divorced, she stopped and took stock of her life and herself. "What a rut I'd dug for myself," she said. "Because I was afraid to enter the dating game, I buried myself in books and snacks. My friend, Carol, screamed at me and shook my tree a bit. 'You're rejecting everyone,' she said, 'without giving them a chance. Every guy out there isn't like your ex.' What do you think I should do?"

"What do you think you should do?" I countered.

"Get out and try again. I've gone on a diet and I've started to exercise. I guess it's beginning to show because I was asked out yesterday. I didn't accept, he wasn't my type, but I think I'll be asked out again. I've noticed I'm walking taller and feeling more confident. Maybe I'll come up with a winner this time. At least I'm going to try. Oh, I bought skis and I'm going to the slopes this weekend. Bought an outfit, too."

Marsha has just entered herself in the dating game. And because she's aware of her total body image, she should come out a winner.

The dating game can be approached from another

direction. What image do the lucky winners of this game project?

When Eric moved to a new city, he became an observer for a few weeks. He studied the newspapers for the places where one could meet a wide variety of women. Then he cased the joints, so to speak, but he wasn't watching the women just yet. He spent time observing the successful men and took note of their clothing and their manners. Then he set about creating an image for himself that was similar but allowed for his individuality. He was smart enough to know that he couldn't be a mirror image of the successful men, but he could use some of their techniques.

To be successful in the dating game, you have to become a Limb Sitter. This means you will both have to create your own opportunities and be able to recognize the opportunities that will come to you.

The Nonclimber will never get to first base in the dating game. He or she will give up without trying. Risks aren't this person's bag, and this is evident in his or her total life-style. This person will be called out on strikes without ever swinging at the ball.

The Trunk Clutcher is full of false starts, but he or she pulls back every time he or she begins. He's always in a position to be tagged out at the bag. Too many false starts can bring disqualifications in the dating game. Each false start ends with a return to the bench. A Trunk Clutcher can end up as a Nonclimber if he doesn't learn to play the game.

While everyone may admire the Branch Breaker, if for nothing else than for the number of times he tries, he's often a loser. The Branch Breaker often chooses the wrong time or the wrong place to run, and he's caught out trying to steal home. He or she can mistake friendliness for a come-on, and he doesn't seem to learn. But even a Branch Breaker can win at the dating game if he learns to modify his approach and take planned risks instead of climbing out too far.

With these preliminary assessments of yourself out of the way, you'll begin to feel more confident about your abilities to attract others. But after the attraction comes the more serious business of forming a relationship. Being part of the group and having a number of relationships is a natural state for people.

The Courtship Strategies

- How did she ever land that guy? He was a great catch. She must know something I don't.

- He's really lucky in love. Half the frat house was after her, but he's the one who pinned her, and they're getting married in June.

Luck or not? Both of these people got what they set out to achieve.

- "It was my state of mind," said Bob. "I planned an active campaign to win her."

- "It wasn't luck," said Sue. "Sure, he was a great catch, but I had to exercise my brain to get him to think I was worth some effort on his part. Strategy counts."

And to set up a courtship strategy, you have to use all your thinking processes. All seven of them can come into play during your courtship quest. The man who marries because it was time for him to marry probably met a woman who devised an effective strategy. The man who meets a woman and decides she's the one for him has to plan a winning campaign. When marriages were arranged, there was no need for a battle plan, but the matchmaker is generally a thing of the past, and today you're on your own.

Rose was the last of her group of sorority sisters to become engaged. She had been involved in her studies, and while she dated, she looked on her dates as friends and fellow students. "It's not that I hadn't thought about marriage, but other things were more important. Then the morning Sue announced her engagement, I thought, 'I want to get married, too.' I went through two pinnings before I found Peter. My vision was very broad at the start."

Broad-scope thinking appears when you come to the realization that you want to get married. "I'm tired of living alone," may be your thought. This kind of thinking may be influenced by what's happening around you. All of your friends and many of your peers may be heading to the marriage altar, and you don't want to get left behind. You may want to get married without a prospective mate in mind. You'll need to use broad-scope thinking to find a general view of the person you want to marry. "A woman. A man. Not too old or too young. Not too tall, short, fat, or thin." You'll have to know what your general likes and dislikes are, and early in the onset of courtship fever, this may be your major concern.

When Rose decided to narrow her view, she applied fine-detail thinking. "One day, it hit me that there were a lot of men, but many of them had qualities I didn't want. I sat down and thought about what I didn't want in the man I was going to marry and then I listed the qualities I wanted. I think some of my friends accepted their proposals just because they were asked. They do a lot of complaining about their fiancé's negative qualities. Peter doesn't have everything I want, but he does have the traits in a man that I need."

Instead of totally relying on broad-scope thinking at the start, shift to fine-detail thinking. This shift may narrow your field somewhat. You've looked at what you want. But what do you need in the man or woman you'd like to marry? While you may want a god or a goddess, there aren't enough of them to satisfy everyone's need. Your needs may be so broad that there is no one who will fulfill all the things you want in a mate. What traits do you want this person to have? Are your choices complementary to your own traits? You can't expect one person to fill all your needs and deficiencies, but finding someone who will help you with your growth is important. You also need to know what traits and habits irritate you and make you want to scream. Make some lists of the negative and positive traits you'd like to have or to avoid in your future mate. Star the ones that you feel must be fulfilled.

A friend once told me about a woman who caught his attention by a very direct means. They live in apartment buildings and can see into each other's kitchens. One day, he looked up and saw her standing at the window. He waved and she disappeared. When she returned, she held up a sign with her phone number printed in large letters. He called her, and now they've set a wedding date for June.

Your vertical ideas may be more subtle than this, but you've got to make yourself visible to use them, for, once you've located the man or the woman of your dreams, your next step is to attract his or her attention. How do you make yourself visible to the other to whom you want to become significant? You can begin by observing their likes and dislikes, and the places where they like to go. You can just happen to arrive at the same place at the same time as you try to use vertical thinking to gain your ends.

Rich was attracted to Jill, one of the girls who worked in his office. So were a lot of the other men, and he couldn't get her attention in a direct way. For nearly three weeks, Rich arrived early at the office and placed a big red apple on her desk. Her curiosity was provoked. When she discovered it was Rich, she accepted his invitation for a date.

Horizontal thinking can give you a plan that brings you to the attention of another by an indirect approach. Any plan you come up with when using this kind of thinking won't find you jumping up and down and waving your arms to attract the attention of another. Planned coincidence is an example of this kind of thinking in action.

John suddenly discovered what Lisa was hinting about when she put her practical left hemisphere to work. The left hemisphere controls orderly, logical thinking. One evening, Lisa talked about the marriage statistics and the pros and cons of marriage. The next evening, she led the conversation into the high cost of living for a person living alone, and how much a person could save with a roommate. The third night, when she steered the conversation into the compatibility needed to form a good relationship, John popped the question. Of course, Lisa accepted with the proper amount of surprise.

Your right hemisphere controls creativity, and after you've been dating your dream for a while, you may find you need a creative way to pop the question, or to get him or her to accept your proposal. Women do make proposals these days. While you may not be a poet, a love letter can always do the trick. Or plan an evening with a romantic flair. An artist is always aware of the subtle touches, and this is where you can try to shine. Flowers, wine, and candlelight can create an atmosphere. Or you could try a series of notes sent through the interoffice mail, or slipped under her door for her to find in the morning. Each note could contain one word of your proposal and you could send one a day.

Contrary thinking can be used during any stage of a courtship. You may be bound by the conventional way of doing things and find you've gotten into a rut with the man or the woman of your choice. You have tried taking your date on walks past jewelry stores and to those romantic restaurants that are conducive to proposing, only to find there's no way short of bluntness to say what you want to say. Try the unconventional. I once heard about a man who put a real diamond ring into a box of Cracker Jacks and sealed it up again. He gave it to the girl he wanted to marry, at a baseball game.

You want to marry him or her, and you're assuming that the

reverse is true. To be successful, you have to use your brain to be aware of the subtle clues the other person has been giving you. In spite of all the thinking and planning you've been doing, if you've been ignoring or misreading clues, you could fall on your face. Contrary thinking is often based on what the other person wants or could be made to want, and not your personal desires.

Before the Honeymoon Is Over

Bob and Sue have been married for twenty years, but to watch them, you'd think the honeymoon was still on. "They sure are lucky." If you ask Bob and Sue if they are still existing under the rules of their honeymoon, they'd probably tell you, "Yes." But their honeymoon rules were different from those of other people.

For many people, the honeymoon is an artificial period in their lives. They get so involved in trying to be what they imagine the other person thinks they are that they hide their real selves. This double dose of imagination can keep you on a high, but you're bound to come down, often with a real crash. There is a moment of discovery—the discovery that you're not the princess he imagined you to be; nor is he the prince you thought he was. Then you discover you can't be the person he holds in his imagination, and the same is true for him.

Bob and Sue have maintained their honeymoon status because they've spent this time looking at the realities of each other. Their fairy-tale romance didn't end abruptly with the words "I do." Nor did they believe in "and they got married and lived happily ever after." Too many marriages have been wrecked on the assumption that courtship is the only time for trials and tribulations and for hard work to achieve happiness. Luck doesn't take over the minute the clergyman pronounces you "man and wife." Bob and Sue employed the six winning strategies to their honeymoon, and they came out ahead of the game.

The first thing they did was to set the Rules of Their Game. No, they didn't think their marriage was a game, but they knew they needed some ground rules. A relationship doesn't last unless there are guidelines that delineate the areas where each person has authority and responsibility. These guidelines may, and even should, be different for each relationship. They need to consider the individual nature of the people involved. Encouragement of each other's growth was one of Bob's and Sue's principal rules. They both realized that a lack of growth causes stagnation, and stagnation brings decay.

Sue enjoyed writing, and she wanted to be a writer. Bob encouraged her efforts and became her critic. Soon they had three small children, and every Sunday afternoon, Bob would take the children to the park so Sue could have a quiet time to write. It took her ten years to achieve her first sale, but after that, she sold many articles and short stories. Twenty years after they were married, Sue wrote a best-selling novel, and she gave Bob half of the credit for her success.

When Bob decided to return to school and change his profession, Sue didn't complain and argue. She realized his growth was leading him in this direction and she willingly tightened the family budget and got a part-time job. Bob's much happier in his new job, which gives him room to expand in the directions he wants.

Other rules that Bob and Sue set in the early stages of their marriage, when many other people are basking in the reflected images from the other, included:

- rules for determining the necessity of purchases, and how they would budget their money.

- rules for dealing with relatives and friends, and how they would satisfy their social needs.

- rules for assessing their rules to see if they should be changed.

- rules for who would be responsible and have authority over the house, the children, the yard, and socializing.

By setting a basic framework, Bob and Sue avoided a lot of confusion about what was coming next and enabled themselves to make planned changes.

By giving each other room to grow, Bob and Sue were considering the Human Factor in their relationship. For two people in a marriage, or in any other close relationship, they're going to have to be themselves in order to have an endurance record. It's hard to pretend you're someone you're not. And in time, cracks will appear in the once-smooth surface. These cracks can become yawning chasms. "He's not the man [or woman] I married anymore," is often said when people approach divorce or separation. The truth of the statement is that he or she is not what you thought they were. Many marriage failures are based on personality molding where one person tries to force the other into an image they have of him or of her.

Laura and Tony ran afoul of this pitfall. When they were married, Laura decided Tony felt her role was to help him through medical school, and then she thought he would help her finish college. Laura worked until Tony finished his internship, and Tony eagerly accepted her help because it meant he had to push less to pay for tuition and he could concentrate on his studies. Three children arrived, and Laura expanded her nurturing role to include them. When Tony opened his office, Laura worked there until he could afford a secretary. When their children were in school, Laura wanted to finish her education. Tony found excuses regarding their financial status, which caused Laura to back down. Tony had cast her in the role of a nurturer, and he was unwilling to change this image. Laura knew she needed some way to use her excess energy, and she drifted into an affair. When Tony discovered this, he was shocked and he left home. Neither of these people fulfilled their images of each other, or their images of themselves. They had left the Human Factor back in the early days of their relationship.

Another rule Tony and Laura ignored was the Rule of Need. When Tony and Laura tried to fulfill their own needs, at different times in their marriage, perhaps they weren't aware that the relationship should be based on a mutual fulfillment of needs in a give-and-take flow. Tony looked on himself as a giver and on Laura as a taker. She felt the same about Tony. They weren't tuned into the real needs of each other, and that their situation had changed during the course of their marriage.

To be successful in a marriage, the Rule of Need must be understood. A person's needs have a way of changing, but often people continue to operate on the basis of their old needs. Sometimes one person will continue to fulfill a need the other person has long ago satisfied.

An elderly patient of mine once remarked that he let his wife make him a complete breakfast every morning because she needed to feel busy and helpful. "It was great when I was working to have a good breakfast, but now that I've retired, I'd rather have juice and coffee," he said.

His wife overheard this comment. "I'd rather not have to cook every morning," she said. "I thought you wanted me to." They both had a good laugh.

The Law of Supply and Demand plays a large role in a marriage, particularly in regard to time. Couples who are still honeymooning often spend as much time together as they can.

What they don't plan ahead for is the time when the demands exceed their available time. A rising young executive may find he has less time for his mate than he likes. The arrival of children may cut a woman's available time for her husband to a minimum. Instead of looking ahead to these times, the honeymooners operate on the assumption that life will always be the same. When time becomes a factor, feelings are hurt because one or the other doesn't have the time to supply the demand from the other.

"Jennie doesn't have time for me anymore," complained Tom. "Since the baby was born, she's either taking care of him, or she's tired. It wasn't like this when we first married."

Tom is looking for Jennie to be his playmate and companion. When I suggested he take up a sport or a hobby, he looked shocked. "I don't want to be with someone else," he said. "Jennie used to play tennis with me every evening. Married people are supposed to do things together."

"And apart," I said. "How do you think Jennie would feel if you had to spend long hours away from home building your career? What would she do?"

"I guess she'd find some way to fill her time," said Tom. "Oh, I see, she doesn't have as much time now, and it may be the same for me later."

On one level, honeymooners look at only one facet of the Compatibility Quotient—their ability to get along with each other. They tend to overlook and excuse faults, which can rub huge craters in their marriage. They ignore the idea that compatibility extends to all facets of their lives. Thus they may find themselves plagued at a later date by such things as:

- Time differential—Jim is a night person, while Marsha is a day person.

- Neatness tolerance—Mary wants her home in perfect order, while Joe doesn't care.

• Social leanings—Janice likes lots of people and
parties, while Mark wants just another couple
and quiet evenings at home.

These areas should be examined early in a marriage, and
compromises should be made. When one person hides
preferences from another, they will surface at a later date and
flow like an erupting volcano over the marriage.

The Principle of Minimax has a definite application during
the honeymoon period of a marriage. This is the time to
become partners and to share the risks. In an effective
partnership, there is equal responsibility, but the risks to each
partner are shared. Often this division doesn't occur because
one partner will expect the other to assume all the
responsibility and all the risk. "If this doesn't work out, I can
always try again," is one way of absolving yourself of
responsibility. "It's all your fault. You didn't try to make it
work," places all the risks on the other person.

Bob and Sue kept their honeymoon going for all those years
because they applied the Principle of Minimax. Each of them
assumed full responsibility for making the relationship work.
Bob could have left Sue to struggle to find time to write, and
Sue could have obstructed his career plans, but when
problems occurred, the person who sensed the problem
brought it into the open and they discussed what was
happening. They didn't try to plaster over the rough spots in
their marriage. They worked together to smooth the lump out.
By doing this, they each assumed half the risks. While they
didn't call what they were doing applying the winning
strategies, this is what they were doing.

If a couple isn't aware of the six winning strategies, they can
lose all control over the longevity of their relationship. After
the honeymoon is over, they may find themselves headed for
divorce.

The Longevity Sweepstakes

• They have a phenomenal marriage record.
How can they be so lucky after thirty years of
living together, when I can't get my second
marriage to run any better than my first?

Relationships of every sort are difficult to sustain on a
long-term, intimate basis. What do those couples who are
winners at the longevity sweepstakes know that the others
don't? Divorce statistics show that nearly 50 percent of all
marriages end in divorce, so when you marry, the odds for your
marriage lasting are just about even. To be lucky, you have to
increase those odds in your favor.

For a married couple to come out on the long end of the
odds, they have to put three programs into effect: goals,
change, and communication. A handy slogan for those
struggling for a long-lasting marriage is, "When goals need to
be changed, communication is a must."

When Steve and Paula were married, they set a number of
goals. They wanted children, to own a house, to be able to send
their children to college, to have money for their vacations, and
to make their retirement years pleasant. As their children
began to near high-school age, Steve saw that his salary was
never going to provide for all the family goals. One evening, he
told Paula that she was going to have to find a job to help the
family realize their goals. Instead of agreeing, Paula felt
threatened and a quarrel began. Their resentment of each
other grew and they ended up in my office for marriage
counseling. The longevity of their relationship was threatened.

I listened to both sides of the quarrel separately. Then I
called the couple in for a joint meeting. "It's clear the two of
you are not going to be able to meet your goals if things
continue as they are."

"I can't imagine myself working," said Paula.

"I can imagine myself dead at fifty from a heart attack because I'm pushing so hard," said Peter.

"You both need to change your images of yourself and each other," I said. "Paula has an image of herself as a wife and mother. If she goes out to find a job with that image, she won't succeed."

"What's wrong with my image?" asked Paula.

"Nothing," I said, "for your present goals. But it looks as though these goals need to be changed. Steve has an image of himself as someone who's reached a dead end. That may also be a faulty image. Sometimes it takes a third person to see what has happened."

I gave Paula and Steve the test to determine their Rejection Index. Paula scored high on avoidance and control. Steve's scores were also high in the same two areas. We talked about these scores, and I sent them home to practice involvement with their problems.

At the next session, Paula and Steve were better able to see what was happening to their marriage. Paula agreed that she had to find a job, and Steve began to see another image of himself—as someone who wanted things to go his way.

"I see what you mean about needing to change my image to get a job," said Paula. "I look and talk like a housewife and mother. It's mainly the way I dress. Steve is the same in a way. He's found a comfortable niche in his office, and he doesn't take as much care of his appearance now."

"We can't afford it," said Steve.

Paula smiled at him. "I'm ready to change my image, but you have to change yours, too. I can't assume all the risks."

"Right," said Steve.

Our next sessions were split sessions. During these times, we worked on creating political personalities based on past successes. Six months after family sessions began, Paula was ready to look for a job. Steve was able to see the way he had boxed himself in, and rather than change jobs, he began to do some free-lance accounting to add to the family's cash flow. The family's goals had changed somewhat, and by changing their images, Steve and Paula had increased the chances of their relationship being a long one.

Couples who are winners in the longevity sweepstakes have learned to set goals. They are aware that unless there is something to work toward, their relationship will go flat. Without goals, life can become a treadmill existence, and this is particularly true in a marriage.

Goals come in two varieties: short-term and long-term. In a marriage, a short-term goal may be something like plans for next year's vacation. A long-term goal may be the purchase of a house or having children. But goals that become rigid, and when it is thought they must be adhered to at any cost, bring problems.

Peter and Grace were planning to spend their vacation in the mountains, as they have every year since they got married. Then Peter's company decided to send him to San Francisco for a conference the week before his vacation was to begin. Peter thought it would be a good idea if they would change their vacation plans and take advantage of the company's payment for his transportation and lodging in San Francisco. He came home excited about the new plan.

"But we've planned for a trip to the mountains," said Grace. "It's too late to change our plans."

"Is it?" said Peter.

"We've always gone to the mountains," said Grace. "I don't want to take a different vacation. Remember how we met there."

Peter and Grace have run into a situation that requires change. Peter is willing, but Grace has gotten into a rut. This incident may be a single-time problem, or it may be the first sign that the vitality and free flow of this relationship is being blocked. In either case, Peter and Grace have a problem which could threaten the longevity of their marriage, and thus there is a need for reassessment and change.

By using the six winning strategies, Peter can help Grace look at the problem and free the plug of resistance to change before the situation becomes irreversible.

Any change that occurs in a relationship, whether it be vacation plans or some more essential area, must be mutually agreed on to make this change work. Because a relationship calls for equal responsibility and shared risks, both parties have to see the need for change. This brings the Principle of Minimax into play. Before this principle will be effective in their case, Grace and Peter will need to consider the Rule of Need, the Compatibility Quotient, the Law of Supply and Demand, the Human Factor, and the Rules of the Game.

Peter and Grace are confronted by what may be a minor difference in their interpretation of the Rules of Their Game. They both agree that there should be a vacation. It's the where that has caused trouble. "Yes, we need a vacation," thinks Grace, "and we have always gone to the mountains." "Yes, we need a vacation," thinks Peter, "and we have this great chance to do something new." The rules haven't changed, but the interpretations of them have.

When Peter decides to change Grace's mind about their vacation plans, he must consider the Human Factor. Is Grace so rigid in her plans that she won't agree to change? Does the new vacation site give him something he wants? A "No" to the first and a "Yes" to the second will help him as he pursues his arguments to change Grace's mind.

Peter must also consider the Compatibility Quotient. What things in San Francisco will Grace enjoy? What things will she miss from their usual vacation in the mountains? By comparing these, he may gain some strong arguments in his favor.

The Law of Supply and Demand can also be used by Peter in his attempts to change Grace's mind. Their usual vacation is two weeks. If they go to San Francisco, although Peter will be attending meetings during the day, they will be able to extend their vacation by a week. Peter can use this fact to help himself convince Grace to make the change. He can also look at their available cash and what their expenses will be for the extended time in San Francisco. Can they afford to make the change? This may be the biggest factor for or against.

In this case, the Rule of Need may be the vital one. Does Peter feel their relationship is becoming stagnant by the lack of change? He and Grace will need to talk about their needs. If Grace is too comfortable with following old habits, there can be a real threat to the longevity of their marriage.

Change is essential to a growing relationship such as marriage. Without change, there is stagnation and death or decay. The beautiful pond in a sylvan setting becomes a scum-covered pool, and the fish that lived there will become extinct if the outlets that permit a free flow of new water are blocked. But change also has its opposite effect. When change is too rapid, and there is no room for reassessment, it becomes chaos. For change to be effective in stimulating growth, it should be planned change. Planned change takes communication.

"He won't talk to me," complained Patti to her friend Tanya. "You and Dave talk all the time. How do you keep him from hiding behind the newspaper and grunting when you ask him to make a decision? I end up making all the decisions, and then he gets upset."

"I try a lot of things," replied Tanya. "It's not easy. Dave would like to hide, too. If one approach doesn't work, I use my brain to find another."

Tanya is very skilled in making the seven thinking patterns work for her. She applies broad-scope, fine-detail, vertical, horizontal, right-hemisphere, left-hemisphere, and contrary thinking to the area of communication in her marriage.

"Three months ago, I hit a real impasse," continued Tanya. "I felt it was time Dave and I started a family, but I also know he's quite comfortable with our life as it is. It took real use of brain power to show him we needed to change our life-style."

When Tanya first started thinking about having a baby, she began pointing out babies and small children to Dave when they were out walking. The usual response was a grunt or a noncommittal, "Yes. The baby is cute." She then let up on broad-scope and turned to fine-detail thinking. She began pointing out to Dave the number of their friends who were starting families. He responded by saying that their friends must have reached the point in life where they needed that change, but he wasn't ready yet.

Tanya moved to vertical thinking by inviting friends who had babies over for dinner. This brought Dave into direct contact with infants, and he began to get involved with observing Tanya holding and playing with babies. When one of their friends had to go to the hospital, Tanya volunteered to take care of their six-month-old baby. This brought horizontal thinking into play. Dave was able to observe what kind of mother Tanya would be, and to help in the care of a baby. He told Tanya that the experience hadn't been as bad as he had thought it would.

Next, Tanya began to use right-hemisphere thinking to influence Dave's thinking. She left articles about children and about pregnancy where Dave could see them. She still got no response, so she put her left-hemisphere to work. She began talking about the practical aspects of having children at their age, and she involved Dave in discussions of what the difficulties of being a parent would be. Still no suggestion from Dave that they should start a family.

When her indirect methods didn't work, Tanya decided to employ contrary thinking. "I want to have a baby," she announced.

Dave laughed. "So do I. I was waiting to see how long you would take to approach the subject directly."

Communication is the third factor in growth that helps

keep a marriage vital and alive. One pitfall to longevity is a
reliance on mind reading. Many people who live together for
many years do become adept at knowing what the other person
is thinking, but there is no guarantee this is true 100 percent of
the time. Open, verbal communication about needs and
desires can be 100 percent effective. Why take chances with
assumptions that may or may not be right?

The other side of talking is listening. How often have you
heard a married person say, "I just turn him [or her] off and
say, 'Yes, dear' a lot." If you don't hear what the other person is
saying, there's a short circuit in your system. Saying "Yes,
dear" to something you haven't heard may land you in divorce
court rather than on the beach when summer rolls along.

That married couple you admire for the longevity of their
marriage communicate, change, and have goals. But then,
they're lucky in their marriage because they care enough to
work hard to achieve success.

7

Luck and the Family Man or Woman

The Lucky Parent

Most people want to be lucky in their career choices, in their love relationships, and they also want this luck to extend to the area of parenthood. Who wants to be a smashing success in business only to have children who bring them bad luck to negate all the good they get from their success? Luck applies to child raising on two levels. One level is for the child and the other is for the parent.

119

- When the police pulled up in front of their house, and the policeman brought Sandi to the door, John and Mary felt like unlucky parents. They couldn't decide what they had done wrong.

- Larry and Rachel beamed with pride when Joni received the Good Citizen award. "We're lucky parents," they said.

These two sets of parents both point toward luck as being responsible for their child's success or failure. Was it really luck that was responsible? Did Larry and Rachel have some magic going for them that John and Mary didn't have? Could it be that Larry and Rachel worked harder to apply the luck-producing techniques to the area of parenting?

Being a successful parent takes hard work, and a little luck can come in handy. Often it is taken for granted that a child becomes an adult, with no thought being given to the steps in between. Commitment to the task is a vital ingredient of the parenting process. If you're not willing to be involved with your child as he grows up, you might as well flip a coin. There's a 50–50 chance he'll grow up to be a lucky adult.

Over the years, many parents have learned that just telling their children what to do, or by being a constant complainer isn't as effective as working to create the images that can be used by their children as they grow older. Children learn best by example. When a parent presents a lucky image to his children, they have a better chance of becoming lucky adults. And there are three stages to creating your lucky parental image: your Rejection Image, your appearance, and your political personality.

- "You'll do as I say," said Tom to his fifteen-year-old son. "I'm your father, that's why."

- "My Bobby is so much smarter than the other kids," said Sherry. "That's why he has trouble getting along with them."

- "I've washed my hands of her," said Susan. "She's brought me nothing but heartache, and I don't care what happens to her."

- "You never do anything right," said Greg to his six-year-old son. "I can't trust you for a minute."

- "Daddy's busy right now," said Mary. "I'm sure he'll want to see your pictures when he has time."

- "You're going to be Mommy's good little boy when the doctor gives you a shot," said Rita. "Then I'll buy you a new toy."

These parents are all using one of the rejection traits in their interaction with their child. When this happens, it affects the child's image of himself. Use of these traits also sets in motion a negative image of the parent in the child's mind. If one of these or a similar statement is used on occasion, it won't affect your child, but a constant application of the rejection traits will make the child feel unlucky.

I see children in my private practice, and not too many months ago I counseled parents who had adopted a child whose behavior and history clearly indicated she had been a victim of most of the rejection traits at some time in her young life. As a result of this early constant rejection, she was unable to trust anyone. "I don't have much luck," is the way Beth put it. "They're going to send me back. I know that." Beth was seven when she told me this.

Her adoptive parents had no thought of relinquishing custody, but it was becoming increasingly difficult for them to deal with her explosive behavior. When I told them Beth was trying to prove she was unlucky because she was convinced she was, they asked, "Why does she feel this way? We're trying so hard."

"It's not your fault," I said. "And you may not be able to undo the damage that's been done. Let's look at Beth and see which of the rejection traits she exhibits and how you can teach her to develop the opposite trait. You're going to have to work on just one at a time. Too much work for her right now will only confuse and threaten her."

Beth had been a battered and often abandoned child. One of the traits she often used was indifference. She acted as though she didn't care about anything or anyone. Empathy is the opposite of indifference, and the first step for her parents to take would be to talk about their feelings and to show that they understood her feelings. This would be the thrust of our therapeutic sessions.

Another rejection trait Beth exhibited was control. She had temper tantrums and used physical action to make other people do what she wanted them to do. Her parents would have to teach her spontaneity by relaxing their need to control her behavior and to set the limits in interactions.

Beth was a whiz at manipulation, and she often used this behavior with her peers. She was convinced no one would like her unless she bought them, so she often used her whole allowance to buy food for her friends, not to mention bringing them into the house and feeding them without asking permission. When she began to steal money to make her bribery more effective, her mother became alarmed. "How do I handle this?" she asked. "Beth denies stealing, but the evidence points to it." Beth needs to learn honesty when dealing with her peers, instead of using manipulation. I encouraged her parents to stop using any hint of bribery in their dealings with her.

Another rejection trait that had become a part of Beth's

nature was avoidance. Every time we approached a subject in therapy that was painful to her, she would change the subject. It took a lot of skill to prevent this, and I wasn't always successful because she was so adroit at this tactic.

While this child represents an extreme case of what can happen when a child is the victim of a constant barrage of rejection traits, playing the game of opposites had a positive effect on her behavior. After a year of extensive therapy, Beth began to feel she was a lucky child, and her parents began to think they might become lucky parents.

The second phase in the development of a lucky image is appearance. Many parents follow the line, "Do as I say and not as I do," in this area. The parent who slumps does not remind his child that he or she should stand tall. The parent who ignores his or her body image by overeating or a lack of exercise is often heard telling his child to watch what he eats, or to be more physically active. Your appearance will affect your child's appearance.

Have you ever watched children play dress-up with their parents' old clothes? It can be an eye opener. Children often assume their parents' mannerisms when they wear their clothes. You can teach your child to have pride in his or her appearance and thus foster a lucky image by showing him your confident posture, a smiling face, a good body image, and how to dress for each occasion.

In order to create an image of yourself as a lucky parent, you have to be able to change your image as quickly as a politician does. Your child will learn to respond to the change in your image, and he or she can learn that a person needs to appear in different ways to accomplish what he wants.

As your child is growing up, one of the important things you can teach him or her is how to communicate. Pay attention to the tone of voice you use when you talk to your child. They may read things into what you're saying that aren't there. Seek to increase their vocabulary by explaining to them the meanings of new words. Above all, strive to keep the lines of communication open between you and your child so he can learn techniques for doing this in his own life.

Being a loving, playful parent can show your child one image. A change to a stern, loving parent will present him with another. If he hears you speaking enthusiastically about your job, he will have a third image. Your child will seek to imitate these images when he is out in the world. By showing your child an image of a lucky person, one who always does his best and who isn't afraid of hard work, your child is likely to follow this example when he creates his own images.

Raising a Lucky Child

Raising a lucky child starts before you actually become a parent. Having children requires a commitment of time and self that is a long one. Few people take the time to determine and evaluate if they are equipped to become lucky parents before they have a child. Before you have a child, the answers to the following questions may help you decide if you have the determination to commit yourself to the job. The questions are based on the six winning strategies you can also use to help your child enter adulthood as a winner.

Laura looked down at her three-month-old baby. "I sure hope you're worth it," she said. "I'd heard babies keep their mothers up all night, but I didn't believe it would happen to me. I haven't gotten more than three hours of sleep in a stretch since we came home from the hospital. If this is how it starts, how much of my time and energy can be consumed?"

- The Rules of the Game—Are you aware of the amount of time and energy, both physical and emotional, that raising a child requires?

"We've got a real problem," said Carol. "Bob wants children and I don't. I never baby-sat. In fact, I ran the other way when I was asked. Bob thinks the fact that I've never liked children will change when the child is ours. I don't see what difference that will make."

- The Compatibility Quotient—Have you been involved in caring for a young child, and were you adept or inept during this experience?

"When I come home from work, I'm exhausted," said Paul. "I find myself screaming at the kids because they are noisy and they want me to play with them. That's the last thing I want to do."

- The Human Factor—What is your capacity for laughter when you're exhausted emotionally and physically?

"We've thought a lot about why we want to have a child," said Sharon. "I think it would be fun to watch a child grow and explore. There are so many things you can teach a child. Maybe I can give him or her the strengths really to accomplish something."

- The Rule of Need—Is your need to have a child based on your desire to nurture and help a human being develop his (or her) full potential?

"I'm not sure we're ready to begin our family," said Greg, "but Marie and I are getting all this flack from both sets of parents. We can't go to either house without being asked when there's going to be a grandchild."

- The Law of Supply and Demand—Are you
  having this baby because of outside pressure,
  which is pushing you to reproduce?

"When the baby comes, it's going to be all hers," said Dick. "I'll bring home the bacon, and she'll take care of the kid. That's the way my parents did it. Boy, you should have heard my father let her know when one of us kids got in trouble."

- The Principle of Minimax—Are you and your
  husband or wife willing to accept 100 percent
  of the responsibility of caring for this child,
  thus sharing the risks?

Few prospective parents answer these questions before they have a child. And, in most cases, they would ignore the answers and choose to reproduce anyway. Many times, the negative responses are negated by the presence of the child, and an average child is the result. But with a little work on the part of the parents, a lucky child who grows into a lucky adult can be the result.

Lucky doesn't mean that your child should be given every material wish either. The lucky child is shown through example and through teaching how to function to his or her fullest potential. This child is able to make decisions, choose goals, and deal with changes as they occur in his (or her) life.

As a parent, your example will be your child's first model. When you make decisions, do you weigh and balance the possibilities, jump in and stick to your choice no matter what, or play around so long that someone else makes the decision for you? Learning to make choices is important for your child, and this can be begun as soon as your child is able to reach for a rattle. As your child becomes older, the choices can be made more difficult, but teaching him how to weigh and balance the possible effects of his decisions will help him as he matures.

Jane took her two girls, ages ten and eleven, shopping for clothes. "I was exhausted when the expedition was over, and part of the time I wished I had just bought their clothes myself. They learned a lot about making choices and about what it costs to live. I gave them each twenty dollars and let them see what they could purchase with that amount of money. Pam went right for the expensive clothes and all she got was a pair of slacks and a top. Karen took over an hour of looking through the sales racks. She got two pairs of slacks and two tops, plus a pair of socks. I had to give Pam the money for the tax. Pam pouted because Karen got more than she did, but she'll remember this lesson the next time we go shopping."

A second area where children need to gain proficiency is at setting goals. Many adults don't set goals and they float through life without achieving very much, but never dipping very low either. The lucky adult knows how to set a goal, how to achieve it, or how to change it if it seems impossible to reach. If your child sees that you have goals, even if it is something simple, like "Today, I'm going to do the laundry," he will have an idea of how to set a goal. If he sees you completing what you said you would, he will see a goal being attained. Of course, if your child hears you setting goals that you never try to achieve, he will feel goals are not very important. And if your child hears you setting goals and aiming to reach them, but constantly falling short, he may also set goals that are impossible to reach.

Denise is a free-lance writer, and her children are receiving lessons about goals from her every day. "I have to write ten pages today," she says. "I'll be in my study until they're done." "No, I can't stop writing to take you to the store for an ice-cream come right now. I have three pages to type. Then we can go." "I have to call the editor today and ask for an extension on this deadline. My co-author hasn't sent me the corrected manuscript." "I'm going to have to change this whole article. The material isn't adequate to carry the number of words they want."

Denise has also shown her children how to set goals when they are doing homework. When they come home and tell her they have a paper to do, she asks, "When?" Then she helps them plan their time so they can meet the deadline.

Change may be the most constant thing about life. Teaching your child how to deal with change can help him become an adult who can both see and initiate opportunities. If your child sees there is no room for change in your life and that you rigidly cling to that which has become outmoded, chances are that he will do the same. This doesn't mean that your life should be filled with ever-shifting currents. You should show your child how to operate with planned change. Letting him see how you apply the six winning strategies will benefit your child when there is a need for change in his life.

When children first learn to play board games, they try to apply the same rules to every game. Many children's board games take this into account, and the rules remain the same while the pictures on the board and the pretend goal change. The child may experience frustration when faced with a game that has new rules, especially when they're trying to play this game by the old rules. What you have to do, in this case, is sit down and explain the new rules often enough that your child understands them.

When I buy a new game for my daughter, we sit down and play a mock game as I read the directions aloud. Then we play a few sample games until we understand the game thoroughly. Only then do we play the new game to see who will win. My daughter has learned a lot from playing games about rules, and one important thing she has learned is that different games have different rules. When I am teaching her how to deal with different situations in life, I often refer to this fact. In this way, she will learn to look for the rules before she plunges into life situations.

Children are fascinated by other people, but many children go through a period of extreme shyness when they turn from other people and cling to their parents. Children also observe how their parents respond to others. The Human Factor deals with how people react to each other, and it is good for a child to begin to socialize at an early age. It is also important for them to recognize the individuality of others, and the more experiences they have with different kinds of people, the more understanding of the Human Factor they will have when they become adults.

For a number of years, Jean held once-a-month soup kitchens. She provided the soup, and anyone who wanted to drop in brought things such as bread, wine, and dessert. Families were included, and her children were exposed and able to interact with a wide variety of adults and children. This phase of their life ended, and Jean didn't realize how much an effect this had had on her children until a teacher remarked that her ten-year-old was able to find his way into any group of children, and he was also able to relate effectively with adults. "He treats everyone like an individual," said the teacher. "It's rare to see a child this age be able to do this."

While Jean didn't look at the Compatibility Quotient of her guests when she planned her Sunday affairs, chances were high that the people she was compatible with would get along with each other. Children also need to learn how to assess their Compatibility Quotient with people and things. How do you handle a situation when your child comes home crying and says, "Johnny doesn't like me"? Or when you arrange for piano lessons only to find he (or she) would be more at home on the baseball diamond. But if you let your child do only what he or she wants to do or be with those with whom there is an instant affinity, he or she may miss out on something or someone that could give them a valuable experience in learning how to get along with others.

"When my kids try something new, I set a time limit for a trial run," said Harry. "If they don't like it after that time has passed, then we sit down and talk about why. I try to do the same thing when they have complaints about another kid. It's good to know why you don't like something, or someone. With people, you've got to be careful, though. Someone can remind you of someone you don't like, only to turn out to be a great guy."

An important distinction the lucky person is able to make is the difference between a need and a want. It's never too early to teach your child how to make this differentiation.

One mother I know responds to her children's complaints of, "I need, I need," by saying, "Is it necessary to keep you alive in some way?" Then they sit down and talk about why the child needs or wants this particular thing. More often than not, the discovery is made that the child wants something rather than needs it. Her children have also learned to identify why they want a particular thing. When they become adults, they will be able to apply the Rule of Need successfully.

Rose and Ray give their children allowances, which are set up on the children's projected expenses for the week. But they expect their children to keep within the limits the children have helped set. If the child overspends, he has to do without until the next week. "They've learned to budget," said Ray. "I wish I had learned about supply and demand when I was a kid. I'm still working on it."

The Principle of Minimax is important for your children to learn. They will be forming relationships throughout their lives, and if these relationships are going to be fortunate, they have to understand about responsibility and risks. The best place for them to learn these is in a family setting and by seeing this principle work with their parents. When they see their mother mow the lawn because their father has hurt his back, or their father pitching in to help with the housework because their mother works, they will come to understand that their parents are willing to assume 100 percent of the responsibility for keeping the family running smoothly. They will also see that the risk of chaos developing is lessened by this strategy.

Children learn best from examples. Their parents are the people they observe most closely. The best way for you, as a parent, to show your child how to have a lucky life is to show him a parent who has one.

Learning Luck

By the time those school bells ring for your child, he should have learned how to learn and thus have learned how to be lucky in his classroom experience. This doesn't mean that you should sit down and teach him how to read, write, and do arithmetic. What it means is that you should attempt to develop your children's skills at the seven patterns of thinking. One of the best ways parents can set up their children for a lucky life is to help them develop skills in this area.

Babies and small children are very much taken with the fine details of everything they see. Watch how they examine a new toy. They look at it closely and turn it around and around to see it from all angles. They touch and they taste just about everything they can reach in their vicinity. A parent can help stimulate this form of learning by making sure the child has plenty of detail in his environment to examine. As the child grows older, the parent can ask the child to describe the details of an object verbally. This verbal addition will help your child in the classroom as he learns the symbols that will be important to his learning.

Broad-scope thinking is often difficult for a child to focus on. Their lives are concerned with learning how small details combine to make a whole, and it is from this direction that broad-scope thinking should be approached. One way to help your child develop powers of broad-scope thinking is to show him pictures that are broad in scope, such as pictures of forests in their fall foliage, which are essentially blurs of color. Another good exercise is to build upon your child's love of detail. Take a flower and make a drawing, beginning with the stem and adding the individual parts. Then place the flower in a garden, the garden near a house, the house on a street, etc. Being able to use broad-scope thinking will be invaluable to your child in the years ahead.

Vertical thinking is seeing what's in front of you. For a child, this learning comes through the discovery of the use of a particular item. A pencil is used for writing. A crayon is used to color. A friend related her child's reaction to the gift of a set of coloring pencils and a coloring book. "Don't have any paper," said the child. "Don't have any crayons." But vertical thinking figures highly in your child's life. This is what helps him learn what the alphabet letters and numbers are used for. So help your child, as he explores his world, to discover what things are used for.

But for children to succeed in school, they also have to be able to see things horizontally. This means seeing other uses for the same things. My friend whose child was confused by the coloring pencils decided to help her child make the shift to horizontal thinking. My friend bought water colors, finger paints, colored pens, chalk, and magic markers. Then she sat down with her child and showed her that each of these items, as well as the coloring pencils and crayons, could be used to color and also to write. She started her daughter on a quest that day that causes her never to look at something and think it has only one use.

As children come closer to the preschool years, their ability to use their right-hemisphere creativity increases. Imagination sometimes seems to get out of control as they use make-believe to learn about life and their relationship to it. Their questions often move from the concrete, "Who?" "What?" "When?" "Where?" "How?" and "Why?" to the more nebulous "What if . . . ?" "What if the sky were green and the grass blue?" These kinds of questions may be unanswerable, but they should be encouraged. Children often lose their imaginative powers to concrete, logical thinking when they go to school. If creative thinking is allowed to lie fallow, your child will have to relearn the techniques involved when he reaches for a lucky life.

The left hemisphere is logical and deals with sequences. You can help your child use this type of thinking before he or she goes to school. Let him or her memorize nursery rhymes and simple songs, and help your child to count by playing counting games with him or her from infancy on. Buy him or her blocks that are different colors and let your child line up all the reds, yellows, blues, and greens. Then let your child count them. Finally show your child how to form sequences of red, yellow, green, and blue blocks in the same row, and then repeat the pattern. Sequencing is an important skill in reading, math, and learning of all kinds. If your child has a good grasp of this skill before he or she goes to school, the child's early education will be much more easily accomplished and he or she will feel successful, thus setting up the lucky feelings in your child.

"What do you mean, I should teach my son contrary thinking?" said Rita. "Mike could give a course in it. He never comes up with the expected answer. The other day, some of the neighborhood kids were arguing about Santa Claus. Some felt he was real, and others said it was the parents. There nearly was a battle until Mike piped in. "Look at it this way. For some people, there's a real Santa Claus, and for some people, there's parents. It's the gifts that really count." He's only six. What do you do with a kid like that? Sometimes he comes up with solutions to problems I didn't recognize as problems until he identified them."

This child has learned to look beyond the ordinary when he seeks a solution to a problem. If he continues to exercise his powers of contrary thought, he'll be well equipped to handle adult life.

You, too, can be a lucky parent and teach your child how to be lucky, if you are willing to spend some time developing your skills and those of your child.

8

The Lucky Life

Toward a Full-bodied Life

Most people aren't content to limit their luck to just one area of life, such as business or marriage. They always hope a little of their luck will rub off on all other areas of living. The couple with the lucky marriage wants this luck to flow into their social experience. The lucky businessman wants a lucky retirement. And everyone wants to have luck with his education.

The luck-producing techniques can be adapted to any area of your life with a little hard work. What about school? Which of these techniques could you apply there? What about the seven thinking patterns, or the six winning strategies, or even the three phases of image creation? Actually, you can devise ways to apply them in any direction you wish.

By applying these lucky techniques to your life, you can become a most lucky man or woman in the eyes of those around you. When you're leading a full-bodied life with its winelike headiness, you'll feel great, and you'll appear lucky to those who sit on the sidelines and only wish.

Ringing Those School Bells

- Jack is a freshman in college and he has a rough course mapped out for himself. He wants to go to medical school and he knows how important his grades during the next four years will be to his acceptance.

- Louise has returned to school after a fifteen-year absence from the classroom. Fifteen years ago, she was a bright student, but she has found the transition from housewife to student to be extremely difficult.

- Brian has had an image as a poor student and a goof-off since he was in third grade. He has just begun his junior year in high school. Last summer, he worked for a vet and he discovered this is what he wants to do for a living. He has changed his mind-set, but he is having difficulty with other people. They are unable to accept the idea that Brian has changed his image.

How can the use of luck-producing techniques help these people make the school bells ring triumphantly for them? They are all willing to take risks and work hard to achieve their goals, but they need to do more than take risks and work. Brian has been a Nonclimber. Louise has been a Trunk Clutcher. Jack is in a position to become a Branch Breaker. They are all aiming to become Limb Sitters.

For Jack, an application of the six winning strategies could help him achieve his goal. But before he begins to put them into effect, he must assess his commitment to his goal of going to medical school. He should consider alternate goals to fall back on should he fail to reach his first goal. Branch Breakers may continue to take risks; they may become Limb Sitters, but there is also the chance that they may become Nonclimbers or Trunk Clutchers. When Jack selects his college major, he should choose one that will give him the ability to succeed if he doesn't achieve acceptance to medical school. In gamblers' language, this is called "hedging your bet," and this is an assurance of winning, even if it's on a small rather than a large scale.

The six winning strategies are: the Compatibility Quotient, the Human Factor, the Rules of the Game, the Rule of Need, the Law of Supply and Demand, and the Principle of Minimax. Let's take a look at how Jack could possibly apply them to himself while he is in college so he will be one of the lucky applicants to medical school.

Jack is aware of the Rules of the Game, one of which is, "Good grades are a must for acceptance into medical school." He has also heard that science majors are more likely to be accepted and to do well, so he has chosen microbiology as his major. Jack also knows that in order to follow the Rules of this Game, he will have to apply himself to his studies, and he may have little time for a social life. He is willing to make this sacrifice.

To have or not to have a social life brings the Human Factor into play. Jack knows that normally he is a social person. He was president of his high-school class for four years, and he dated a number of girls. He doesn't want to give all this up, because he feels that retaining some sociability will help him become a better doctor, but he also knows he will have to be careful not to let this side of his character assume control.

In order to assure himself of success, Jack needs to use the Rule of Need for an evaluation of his reasons for wanting to be a doctor and what needs this career choice will fill. His reasons may not have an important bearing on his decision, but if he knows them, he will also be able to decide when his needs aren't being fulfilled by the course of study he has chosen. Periodically, he will have to reassess his needs so he can see if he chose wisely. Unwise choices are seldom lucky.

Along with the Rule of Need, Jack will have to look at his Compatibility Quotient. During the summers, he can test his affinity with medicine by taking jobs that are health-related. Many people are attracted to medicine because it is a prestige field, and it almost automatically seems to assign luck to the holder of its degree. This won't happen if Jack should discover after all the long, hard years of school that he made the wrong choice.

Jack's success at following the Rules of the Game will determine his luck with the Law of Supply and Demand. There are only a limited number of medical-school openings every year, and the competition for these slots is heavy. Jack's grades will tell if his demand will be successfully met.

When Jack chose microbiology as his major, he knew if he wasn't selected for a medical-school slot, he could still have a medically related career. In doing this, he was applying the Principle of Minimax. This would insure his eventual success in life, though it might not fulfill his original goals.

In Louise's case, the seven thinking patterns will be the most valuable aids in producing luck as she returns to school. The first thing she will need to do is to determine the forms of thinking she most regularly uses. The process of education requires many types of thinking, and the forms Louise will need most are dependent on her selection of a major. If she chooses a math or a science major, she will need strength in

fine-detail, vertical, and left-hemisphere thinking. For an arts
or a letters degree, broad-scope, horizontal, and right-hemisphere thinking will best suit her needs. Contrary thinking is
applicable to either course of study.

By answering these questions, Louise can get an idea of her
present patterns of thinking, and she will then be able to use
the exercises designed to stimulate and strengthen those areas
where she is weak.

- Do I look at things as a whole picture?
  (broad-scope thinking)

- Am I concerned about finding all the details
  when I examine information of any sort?
  (fine-detail thinking)

- Do I see only the obvious when I look at
  pictures or when I read? (vertical thinking)

- Am I able to discover with ease the peripheral
  views and meanings in the things I read and
  see? (horizontal thinking)

- Am I logical and do I have a good memory for
  facts and figures? (left-hemisphere thinking)

- Am I fascinated by words and their uses and
  meanings? (right-hemisphere thinking)

- Am I able to see the unusual approach to
  problems? (contrary thinking)

After her assessment, Louise should refer to the appropri-
ate exercises for the development of strength where she is
weak in using thought patterns. By doing this, she will increase
her luck and help herself successfully navigate her course of
education.

For Brian to appear lucky, he needs to change his image,

and to make this change believable to other people. He will have to work hard to negate the image he had earlier created for himself. In creating a new image, Brian's appearance will count. He will have to cultivate a more serious expression and watch his posture to see that they project his image as a serious student rather than as a fool. His choice of clothing can give him an assist in the creation of this new image, and once people get over questioning and doubting his change, they will begin to accept the new Brian, if he has few lapses.

Brian has a reputation of being a Nonclimber. He had cultivated the image of class fool nearly to perfection. In fact, he nearly blew his luck because he had begun to believe this image of himself. In order to create an image of a good student, Brian will have to put his verbal skills into high gear. He will have to learn how to ask intelligent questions, how to respond in a thoughtful rather than a flip manner. Grammar, pronunciation, and his choice of words will be important. If Brian persists, he will be able to project his new image successfully and take another step along the road to being lucky.

Climbing the Social Ladder

Some people seem to be lucky socially. They are surrounded by friends, and their lives are full of interesting diversions. These people are fortunate in their social network. You've all seen the person at a party who is in the center of the group. Or there is the man or woman who you always call when you're having a social affair. "He makes a party happen," you may comment. "She has such great ideas about what to do." These are the people who are at the top of the ladder in your particular society. They are the catalysts who make things happen, and everyone wants to be with them.

On the reverse side, there is the person no one wants to be around. "He's such a wet blanket. When he walks into a room, he smothers all the action." "I wouldn't invite her to my party. She'll turn it into her affair. She just can't help taking over, and she has a real talent for making me feel like a failure." "He'll turn your party into chaos. He has no idea of what's enough."

While no one's social life is one continual party, often the way you act at a party is a key to your behavior in other areas of life. The lucky person is also lucky socially, and the reverse is also true. Few people stop being themselves when they enter a different setting. The luck-producing techniques can be used to help you climb the social ladder and make this area part of your attainment of the full-bodied life.

From the time you're a child, you're constantly encouraged to smile. People cluster around a baby, and when he smiles, they become excited. A baby soon learns that a smile will gain attention. But a baby also learns that a frown or tears will gain attention. Whichever facial expression gives him the most attention may be the one he chooses later in life. It becomes a habit. But as adulthood approaches, a frown no longer gains attention; it causes rejection, and the person who learned this behavior as an infant establishes a spot at the bottom of the social ladder. If the person is you, you don't have to remain there. Perhaps a change of image is in order.

If you're the low man on the social ladder, check your Rejection Index. But don't stop there, and don't rely completely on your responses to the questions. Ask someone else to help you determine where you stand. You may think you are acting one way when you're not. Often the person who is easiest to fool in this area is yourself. Once you've identified your rejection traits, play the game of opposites. You may not see a change overnight, but if you persist, it will come.

Once you have begun changing your image by eliminating your rejection traits, don't forget your appearance. I know a man who is very much avoided even though he can be bright and funny because he talks to everyone with his eyes shut. His posture is also that of a defeated man. Another man I know is avoided because he mumbles. It's impossible to carry on a conversation with him because you have to strain to hear what he's saying. One of my neighbors is the first person invited to a cookout, but she's left out of other gatherings because everyone's afraid she'll show up in jeans at the formal dinner they planned.

To help yourself appear lucky in the social game, assess your physical appearance. It's important from head to toe. If you're overweight, go on a diet. Many times people are afraid fat guests will eat them out of house and home. Suppose you're the awkward type who plays havoc with your host's antique Japanese vases. Take a ballet course, or if you think that's too sissified, a judo course might help you gain control of those awkward movements.

Your political personality is important to your social luck. A Nonclimber doesn't get involved in the social game. He may not be invited, or he may choose to stay away. The Trunk Clutcher and the Branch Breaker are guaranteed poor luck in social affairs. The Trunk Clutcher feels threatened when things aren't as they always were, and he or she demands a formal set of rules that must be strictly kept so that he or she can interact socially. "How do I act?" he asks. "What do I do? This isn't at all like Mary's party." He or she may block the way for all those gathered behind them on the social ladder. Excitement is what a Branch Breaker brings to a social situation, and this excitement often borders on chaos. He or she isn't content to leave things the way they are. Change, change, and more change can often cause this partygoer to fall. It usually isn't just the Branch Breaker who falls, but also everyone on the social ladder with him.

If you find yourself classified as one of these types of social climbers, try a change of image. You may be surprised at the results. Consult your past for a successful pattern to imitate.

The host or hostess with the most are skilled in using their heads. Thinking patterns can bring luck in social situations, and they really help when you're planning your own social affair. Use broad-scope thinking to set the general tone at your party or dinner. Then add fine-detail thinking to plan the specifics.

Vertical thinking will identify the obvious things you should do to prepare, while horizontal thinking will give you a chance to discover where things may go wrong and to take steps to prevent calamity. Use your left hemisphere when you're buying food and drink. It will help you make sure you have enough. Right-hemisphere thinking can help when you're decorating or planning entertainment. Contrary thinking will add those unusual touches that can give your party a flair and make it a smashing success.

Mary seldom has a party, but when she does, everyone she knows hopes to be invited. Contrary thinking is very much a part when Mary plans a party. A few years ago, as she approached her thirty-fifth birthday, Mary read an article that said after a woman reached thirty-five, she often began a new life. Mary had been reading about midlife crisis and how people were often around thirty-five when this began. She decided to celebrate her birthday by holding a wake for herself. Her plans were complete from the black-bordered invitations to the reading of a will, as well as presentation of gag gifts to her friends at the end of the evening. While this may sound a bit macabre, the party was the talk of the town for months afterward. People approached Mary on the street and asked to be invited to her next party. Other people called Mary and asked her to plan their parties. She soon had a thriving business.

You can employ the six winning strategies at any point in your climb up the social ladder. They are especially effective when you're the new kid on the block, or when you're itching for a change in your social life-style.

The Human Factor includes you and those people you wish to have in your social circle. While you may want to exclude yourself from these deliberations, this won't be a lucky choice. You have to know your skills at interaction before your barge into a group and find yourself ejected. You should wait for an invitation or try to make friends with just one person in the group you've chosen. This is a smart way to use the Human Factor because, if you're able to get along with one member of a group, the chances are high that you will feel comfortable with the others.

When you choose one person in a group to test the waters, you are employing the Compatibility Quotient. You should choose the person you think you will feel most comfortable with. For example, if you're a lamb, you wouldn't want to be part of a pride of lions. This may be a good idea theologically, but you could find yourself eaten alive.

One reason for this happening is that you haven't learned the Rules of the Game for the group you want to enter. This social circle may have rules that are contrary to your inner nature. You'll only be unhappy trying to play a social game by rules that don't fit you.

Before you join a group, you should look to see if this group can fulfill your needs for social interaction. The husband of one of my patients joined a church choir to give himself a social outlet and a chance to develop friendships. There were a few things wrong with his choice. The choir liked to have parties where alcohol was served, and this man was anti-alcohol. They were also into hikes and other physical activities, and this man's choice of an evening with friends was to get involved in intellectual discussions. Assess your needs before you choose your social mates or you can find yourself completely out of step.

The Law of Supply and Demand may influence your choice of a social group. You may live in an area of low population density where your choice is limited. You may also want to belong to a certain group, no matter what the cost to you. This is a choice you will have to make after you've considered the alternatives.

It may be easier if there are two of you trying to break into a social group. This employs the Principle of Minimax. An interesting side effect may occur: By joining with another person to enter a particular group, you may find that the two of you have formed the core of your own group.

Painting Retirement Golden

Many people face retirement with the feeling that luck has deserted them. Others use these years to continue their winning streak. Still others are able to accomplish things they weren't able to do during their working years.

Attitudes about retirement are important. There are many stories told about men or women who use their retirement years to become successful, although they weren't before. It takes a full use of the seven thinking patterns to make retirement golden. If you're approaching this time of life, apply the double patterns and add a touch of contrary thinking to keep things interesting.

When Edna retired to Vermont, she was employing what appeared to others to be contrary thinking. But to her, she was going home. "Why go to Florida when you like snowstorms?" she thought. Edna turned her retirement into a Yankee pattern of thrift and ingenuity. If you were to meet her, you'd never think she was in her late seventies. Besides contrary thinking, she applied the other thinking patterns to make her retirement a pleasure for herself.

When Edna picked the house that became her retirement home, she used a combination of vertical and horizontal thinking. She had been left the house as part of a family estate; the house was on the far side of a lake. Her brother's house was on the other side, but his daughter lived near Edna's house. Edna traded houses with him, and her new house was near a main road so she would be sure she could get to town when the winter storms arrived.

As she furnished her house, she used both broad-scope and fine-detail thinking. Attempts had been made to remodel the old house, and the first thing she did was remove the wall-to-wall carpeting and restore the wooden floors to their original finish and pattern. This meant parqueting the dining-room floor, and she did it all herself. She combed the attics of relatives and began refinishing and restoring furniture. When you walk into her home today, though there are electric lights, you feel as though you have stepped into the past, so complete is the picture she has created.

With typical Yankee ingenuity, Edna turned her skill at restoring furniture into a business venture. She now earns enough money to supplement her retirement pay and to allow for the extras she enjoys. Edna used both right- and left-hemisphere thinking to make her business a success. There are many people who refinish furniture, but there are few who are able to cane. This process is tedious and requires nimble fingers and a sense of design.

If when you retire, you create an image of a doddering reject, that's what you'll become. Look at Grandma Moses, the painter, who became a famous artist during the years when many people are tottering off to a nursing home. You have to practice keeping your image intact, and perhaps creating a new image or two to use during your retirement years. Thus you can become successful at keeping your life full.

When Mary returned to Northern Ireland to spend her retirement years, she didn't expect to gain prestige. She was just going home where she could stretch her Social Security payments and help her family by caring for her older brother. Not long ago, Mary was selected as "Woman of the Year" for her county in Northern Ireland, and her prestige was not connected with the trouble there. This was quite an achievement for a woman who had been a housewife and mother after she married a man with three children.

Mary didn't change her image completely to win this award. Instead, she expanded her efficient, nurturing-mother image to the community instead of to the home. She organized and helped run a drop-in center for the elderly where meals were served and arts and crafts programs offered, and she ran a program of day and week trips for the elderly. Not content with this, she took over the youth group of her local church and helped organize activities and day trips for twenty to thirty teen-agers.

My cowriter went on one of the day trips for teen-agers, and she felt she wanted to get out at the first crossroads. "The noise level was unreal, but Mary kept her composure in the midst of all this. I'll never know how."

Before you retire, a look at the six winning strategies can help you appear lucky in the eyes of others during your retirement. They may even want to emulate your success. By using these strategies, you can set a master plan that allows for many possibilities.

Keith wasn't content only to bask in the sun, so he chose his retirement site so he could employ the Compatibility Quotient. It's true, he did move to Florida, and while he does bask in the sun when he has time, he also uses his two lifelong hobbies to make his life full. One of his hobbies is creating Civil War dioramas for a local museum, and the other is giving lectures on deep-sea marine life. On some days he is busier than he was before he retired, but he is now involved in doing things he enjoys.

Lana and Toby are employing the Principle of Minimax to make their retirement enjoyable. They had both been English teachers earlier in their lives. Now they are using their skills to write mystery novels. "He does the action and description," said Lana. "I dream up the plots and the conversation. It's a lot of fun and also brings in some welcome money. In a pinch, either of us can do the other's job. Last year when I had a cataract removed, Toby jumped in and completed a book that had a deadline. He didn't do a half-bad job with my half of the book."

Sarah knew herself very well, and so when she retired, she looked at the Human Factor. "I don't like to be alone," she said. "I never have. Jim would like to be off fishing somewhere, so when we looked for a retirement site, we had to find a place that would suit us both—people for me and a fishing lake for Jim."

Scott had been self-employed all his life, and didn't choose to participate in Social Security. His retirement had to include a part-time job for himself. Thus he employed the Rule of Need. He found a spot in California where he takes care of a wealthy family's garden in exchange for a small house for himself.

When Bob and Laura retired, they stayed in their own home and filled the Law of Supply and Demand. Just before they retired, their grandson came to live with them while he attended college. He remarked about the scarcity of houses for students in the vicinity, and he persuaded them to rent out their empty bedrooms to some of his fellow students. Bob and Laura found they enjoyed having young people around, and though their grandson has graduated, they still rent out rooms to college students. Now Laura's busy baking and cooking for assorted young people, and Bob is their resident engineering consultant.

As you look at the Rules of the Game for retirement, you will discover there are no rules. It will be up to you to create your own, and with a little bit of luck, your retirement can be just as fulfilling, and perhaps more so, as the years that went before.

Throughout your life, you can employ the luck-producing strategies in nearly every situation in which you find yourself. When you do, you'll see people smile and point to you. "He's certainly lucky." "She has the longest winning streak I've ever seen."

9

Keeping
the Winning
Streak
Alive

Running Out of Luck

Even the most lucky person in the world can run out of
luck. There's the person who reaches the top in show
business, only to have his run come to an end. Dick Clark's
"Variety Show" was canceled on him even though the show was
making money. Then there's the successful businessman who
suddenly vanishes, or who plunges from his office window
because luck seems to have deserted him. Closer to home is
the couple you thought had everything going for them; you

envied their luck. You're shocked when you hear he's lost his job, she's having an affair, and their kids have been arrested for peddling drugs at the local high school. Many people have extreme reverses that shock everyone who knows them. Some of these people fold, but others pick themselves up and give it another try.

Who are the people who run out of luck? you may wonder. Are there special signs you could be on the lookout for so you can determine when your luck is coming to an end? While just about everyone can run out of luck, there are three types of people who seldom get up and try again. There are also a number of psychological pitfalls that can make you think your luck has run out. By being aware of the unlucky personality profiles and the psychological pitfalls, you may be able to nip your fall from luck at the start.

The first type of luck loser is the Dependent. He or she can take three paths in his search for indecision. Dependent No. 1 has ridden to success on someone else's luck. This Dependent person may appear lucky to others, but he doesn't know what to do with his luck. He stands and hopes someone will tell him what to do. He or she can be seen in the person who suddenly reaches the top and just as suddenly disappears.

Dependent No. 2 has abrogated his rights to his luck. He worked hard on the way to the top, but once he arrived, he was content to drift and let others make the decisions that would insure his future success.

When Buddy was on his way up, he worked hard. He did all the scrambling to make his rock group a success. He found the gigs, arranged the music, negotiated the payments, and often he had to go out and collect them. The spotlight turned on him and his group, and they soon reached success. By this time, Buddy had accumulated a manager, an accountant, a lawyer, and an arranger. Buddy relinquished control of his future to these people for fees, which left him with less money than he thought. While he basked in the spotlight, the popularity of his group began to slip. Buddy waited for the experts to bail him out, but they left before the group reached the bottom. Buddy was too discouraged to try again.

Dependent No. 3 doesn't depend on people. He chooses drugs or alcohol to keep himself from making decisions. At the slightest hint that his luck is slipping, he reaches for the pillbox or the bottle, instead of working to change his luck.

Grace was thought of by her neighbors as the luckiest woman alive. Her husband seemed to adore her, and her children were dream children. What the neighbors didn't see was that Grace discovered her lucky marriage was disintegrating. Grace began to drink instead of working to improve her marriage, but this only seemed to be an escape. She went on to lose everything.

Dependency is a passive state leading to a downhill slide. By giving up independence of action and decision-making, the Dependent loses his finger on the pulse of his future. This is the easy way out. Decisions are hard to make, and they involve a valuable commodity—self-investment. This doesn't mean you can't delegate authority to others, but it does mean you have to retain your veto powers. The Dependent doesn't retain these powers.

The Egotist belongs to the second class of luck loser. While the Egotist may use many methods to prove he is better than anyone else, there is only one form. No one can do what the Egotist does better, and he doesn't hesitate to let it be known. He may have help reaching the top, but he goes out of his way not to acknowledge this help. Somewhere along the way, he acquires an "I've got it made" attitude and soon this becomes "I did it myself." After a while, a ruthlessness creeps into his dealings with people and he begins to use them. He may give money to a college or institution, but this is done to keep the spotlight on himself, not for the good it will do others. He doesn't want to share the spotlight with anyone. His luck is often slowly eroded by the people he trod upon.

I met a self-made millionaire when he was donating money to a charity with which I was involved. He was the speaker at the banquet, and he spoke of how hard he had worked to achieve success, and how he had been able, through his own efforts, to create lucky breaks. I was much impressed and agreed that he was lucky. I also wished I had his kind of luck until later that evening. Then I learned that his wife was being treated for alcoholism and that his son had committed suicide.

The Dreamer is the third class of unlucky fellow. There are two types of Dreamers. You may know Dreamers who have never reached the top. This is the passive Dreamer, who exists on fantasy trips. His position in life is to be found on cloud nine, where he's busy spinning dreams out of fluff. He often speaks about what he should have done to achieve success, or what he could do now to reach the top, but he has more fun planning what to do than putting his plans into action. There's a certain amount of wistfulness about the passive Dreamer. "If I had done _____ I would have been rich and successful," he says with a sigh.

The active Dreamer is one who rides his luck to the top. Once he's there, he often buries his head in the sand. "I'm here," he says. "Aren't you jealous?" He doesn't act in a manner that is likely to keep him there.

Larry actively courted and won the girl most of his classmates wanted to marry. He and his wife left for their honeymoon in a blaze of happiness and to the tune of "He's so lucky." But two years later, Larry found himself in divorce court. Once the minister had said, "I now pronounce you man and wife," Larry had stopped working to make his marriage a success.

Active Dreamers often have just one goal. Once they have achieved that goal, they don't set another. After all, they got what they set out to get.

The Dependent, the Egotist, and the Dreamer are all classes who sooner or later run out of luck. They all fall victim to one or more of the psychological pitfalls that help bring them down from up.

The Psychological Pitfalls

Many people reach the top only to find their luck has deserted them. This may or may not be true, but their attitudes are what make it so. What makes the lucky person suddenly become devoid of the very qualities he had just a short time before? For some reason, the winning streak has run into a roadblock.

To say it's all in your head may sound simplistic. It may be hard for you to admit that you're your own worst enemy. You may find it easier to blame your failure on something or someone outside yourself.

Failure affects many people in a peculiar way. "One success does not make you successful" is a common thought. But one failure makes many people feel they can't do anything right.

Lois came into my office and announced she was a failure. "I can't do anything right," she said. "I'm so unlucky."

While we talked, I discovered that Lois had deemed herself a failure because she thought she had failed at mothering. Then I pointed out to her that she had successfully raised three children, and that taking on the fourth may have been taking on more than anyone could manage. Her fourth child was adopted. This child had been a battered child who had lived in a multitude of foster homes before Lois and her husband adopted her. On the strength of a single failure in a single area of life, Lois was ready to call herself unlucky. The rest of her life was full of successes.

During our sessions together, Lois and I talked about her successes: the writings she had published, her recent graduation from college with a B.A. in English and a 3.6

average, and the growing maturity of her three other children. By weighing these successes against the failures in her life, Lois was able to see that she was on the plus side of the scale. After four months of exploration, Lois was able to realize she was successful, and, indeed, she was a lucky person.

If you make too many false starts, you can also come to consider yourself unlucky. False starts are often the results of poor planning and faulty information. Taking a plunge into an icy pool can wake you up. It can also bring cramps that cause you to flounder and perhaps drown. When you have made a number of false starts, you may begin to believe you will never get anywhere. This attitude can invade your thinking to the point where it becomes true and you will consider yourself a failure.

Emotional bankruptcy is a group of luck-breaking attitudes that are often found together. This syndrome shows a loss of dreams, a feeling of emptiness, a desire to escape, arrested development, and stagnation. They don't all have to be present for you to be suffering from this syndrome.

Jason was a successful writer, but he developed a giant-sized writer's block. "I just can't write," he said. "I no longer know where my writing's going, and I'm not sure I have anything to say. I used to dream of making it big as a writer, and I haven't done badly. I support myself, but lately, everything I do is awful. I spend my time doing everything except write. When I go into my study, I want to escape. I'm afraid I've dried up. The words don't flow the way they used to. I'm writing the same thing over and over. It's not getting me anywhere. All the joy is gone from writing."

Jason exhibits most of the symptoms of mental bankruptcy. He no longer has a dream or a goal for which he's headed. It may be that he has reached his initial goal, and now must set a new one. In fact, all the symptoms of this syndrome can be connected to the achievement of goals. Unless a goal is within reach, a person can't feel a sense of accomplishment. If the goal is too distant or too ethereal, by the time you reach it, you may feel there is nothing left to do. Sometimes the goal can seem so far away that ennui sets in, and you will suffer from a case of arrested development wherein you are unable even to reach for the success that is within your grasp. You have stagnated, and thus mental bankruptcy is the result.

- "I don't deserve the good luck I have," said Toby. "I can't handle it."

- "I'm not lucky," said Sue. "I don't want to be up here. I didn't use other people to get where I am."

Guilt is a big luck ender. Many people feel guilty when they reach success and other people haven't. Our society is full of devices that help people strive for success and at the same time make them feel guilty for succeeding.

This is particularly true when it comes to making money, but love also comes in for its share of guilt inducers. The assumption is that the lucky person has denied other people their share of luck. You're told that if you succeed, someone has failed as a result. You're made to feel it's wicked to have more than someone else thinks you should have. Self-interest is called a sign of greed. And, of course, you're told greed is wrong.

Some people feel that success must make them feel guilty. If it doesn't, they think there is something abnormal about their attitude. Even if their luck is based on hard work, they feel they're getting more than their fair share and that this isn't right. Yes, they do seem to have more than their share of luck, but to remain guilt-free, they have to balance this against the amount of work they have done to make this luck.

I overheard a conversation in a restaurant a short time ago that illustrates this point.

"I feel so damned guilty," said one woman, "All my friends are getting divorced and my marriage is thriving."

"But you work hard to make your marriage stay alive," said the other woman.

"I know that, but it doesn't stop the guilt. I keep thinking, 'What have I done to deserve my luck?' I'm no better than my friends. I'm afraid I'll do something to turn my marriage into a failure just because everyone else is failing in theirs."

The psychological pitfalls of failure, false starts, emotional bankruptcy, and guilt can cut your winning streak short. To avoid these, you need to develop plans to fight them, and what better methods are available to you than the luck-producing techniques we have been discussing?

Don't Throw Good Fortune Away

In order to keep your winning streak alive, you should be aware of how you got to the top in the first place. Your goals, your use of the luck-producing techniques, and your ability to grow through change are what are responsible for your rise, not some vague rise of a magic wand. When you feel yourself falling into one of the psychological pitfalls, and thus tossing your luck away, you can halt this process in three steps.

The first step is to re-evaluate your goals. Where are you heading? Is it possible to get there? Is there a goal you can set that will take a shorter time, and perhaps move you closer to your final goal? Is the goal you set last year, or yesterday, the one you want today? A periodic reassessment of your goals is one step that will keep your luck effervescent.

After you have reassessed your goals and devised new ones, you will need to look at the luck-producing techniques and see if you are using them effectively.

The Seven Thought Processes

• Broadscope thinking—Barry kept his winning streak alive in his business career by doing research that discovered how many people in this country enjoyed Chinese food. He convinced the heads of his food chain to stock fresh Chinese vegetables.

• Vertical thinking—Trudi taught her children how to recognize their good fortune by pointing out to them just how often they succeeded instead of reminding them of their failures.

• Fine-detail thinking—Joyce kept her romance alive by noticing the fine details of her fiancé's likes and dislikes, such as how he liked his coffee and how he wanted his socks folded.

• Horizontal thinking—Don didn't put all his eggs in one basket educationally. With his double major, he has a choice of jobs.

• Right-hemisphere thinking—Ralph has a fortunate social life, and it should continue because he's always looking for new things to explore.

• Left-hemisphere thinking—Anna's practical mind has given her money and pleasure during her retirement. The calls for her to go with families on vacations around the world to look after their children keep her life full and busy.

• Contrary thinking—Janice received an award at the hospital where she works for discovering why the IVs were finishing too quickly.

Everyone else blamed the other person, but she looked at the adjustment valve and found there was no bridge to prevent the valve from moving if the patient was restless.

The Six Winning Strategies

- The Rules of the Game—Jean and Joe have kept their marriage alive for fifty years by paying attention to the goals and rules they made during the early years of their marriage.

- The Human Factor—By realizing that each of her children is an individual, Loretta has seen her children develop strengths and qualities that will help them succeed in life.

- The Compatibility Quotient—Marcy is using her liking for food and cooking as she works toward a degree in nutrition.

- The Rule of Need—Peter recognizes his need for physical activity as he plans his social life to include such sports as skiing and tennis.

- The Law of Supply and Demand—When David retired, he knew he had a heart condition, so he looked for an area that could supply him with the medical facilities his health might demand.

- The Principle of Minimax—Josie knew she was deficient in her ability to see practical details, so she chose Max to be her partner because this was one of his skills.

The Three Phases of Image Changing

• The Rejection Index—Before he re-entered the dating game, Sam checked his rejection traits and played the game of opposites. He does these things each time his luck seems to falter.

• The Appearance Gauge—Stella is showing her children how to be lucky by showing them a mother who keeps an eye on her appearance. She shows them how to balance diet and exercise to maintain a good body image. They also discuss fashion and how you can look good and still keep within your budget.

• The Political Personality—All of Jason's teachers look on him as a fortunate student, and they are always willing to give him extra help. He maintains this opinion because he has learned how to shift his images to those that the teachers want to see.

After you have explored these techniques, then look at your need to change how, where, or when you have been applying the luck-producing techniques. You may find that a change is necessary. Don't be afraid of change. You can control it, and change is an essential ingredient of growth. It's the growing person whom other people see as lucky, not the person who's sitting still.

Index